CATCH THE VISION

CATCH
THE
VISION

Roots of the
Reformed recovery

John J. Murray

EVANGELICAL PRESS

EVANGELICAL PRESS
Faverdale North, Darlington, DL3 0PH, England

e-mail: sales@evangelicalpress.org

Evangelical Press USA
P. O. Box 825, Webster, New York 14580, USA

e-mail: usa.sales@evangelicalpress.org

web: http://www.evangelicalpress.org

First published 2007

British Library Cataloguing in Publication Data available

ISBN-13   978-0-85234-667-9   ISBN 0-85234-667-0

Printed and bound in Great Britain by Biddles Ltd, King's Lynn, Norfolk, UK.

To my children,
Anna and Andrew with Kirsteen
and grandchildren
James, Calum and David,
heirs of a precious heritage

Contents

Illustrations

Acknowledgements of illustrations used, with kind permission

Page 40:	Mr Jim Eshelman and Grace BC
Page 42:	Mr H. Grier
Pages 46, 49, 58, 76, 85:	Evangelical Library
Pages 24, 35, 39, 60, 108, 118, 148:	The Banner of Truth Trust
Page 66:	Evangelical Movement of Wales
Page 92:	Dr James I. Packer
Page 131:	Rev. James Frew
Pages 128 and 137:	The Archives of Montgomery Library at Westminster Theological Seminary, Philadelphia, PA

Whilst every effort has been made to obtain necessary permission regarding publication of photographs, if any have been inadvertently omitted please let us know and acknowledgement will be made in any subsequent reprints.

Preface

I believe that a significant change came about in the history of the church in the United Kingdom in the middle decades of the twentieth century. It was by and large a recovery of something that had been a reality in the church in past generations. Step by step men were led to see what was missing in the type of Christianity that prevailed for the first half of the century and began to direct their minds back to the glories of past eras.

It is instructive to trace the various strands which were woven together in the providence of God to bring about the recovery. In most cases it was the discovery of some treasure of Christian literature from a spiritually favoured age that set the person on the course he took. We find in the unfolding of history how the flame that burned in the heart of a man of God at one time is years later rekindled in another — as happened in the case of George Whitefield being directed to Henry Scougal's *Life of God in the Soul of Man,* and in the way that the young Charles Haddon Spurgeon discovered the writings of the Puritans.

The purpose of this work is to trace these providential links in the men and the books that set in motion a recovery of the vision. I go back to the harbingers of a new day, looking at the stirrings in university Christian Unions and the raising up of such men as W J. Grier, A. W. Pink and E. J. Poole-Connor. The central place is given to the influences that shaped the message and ministry of the leading figure in the recovery, Dr D. Martyn Lloyd-Jones. Woven around that ministry I trace the origins of the Evangelical Library through Geoffrey Williams, and look at the men who initiated the Puritan Conference, particularly James I. Packer. Finally I examine the steps that led Iain Murray to the founding of the Banner of Truth Trust and brought Professor John Murray into the subsequent Ministers' Conference work.

I do not attempt to give the complete life story of the men concerned but merely a sufficient part of it to show the way in which each of them came to grasp the vision and to advance it in their day. I have had the privilege of knowing these leading figures in the recovery of the Reformed vision and working alongside them. This *personal* contribution to the history of these fascinating decades is both a thankful remembrance of what I believe was 'a work wrought of God' and an expression of gratitude for what I learned from the lives and writings of those men that are featured here.

I would like to thank in particular the Rev. Iain Murray for extending to me the invitation to join the Banner of Truth Trust team in 1960 and to express my indebtedness to all the colleagues I have worked alongside for their stimulation and support in the furtherance of the Reformed cause. I had a connection with Evangelical Press in its beginnings, giving editorial assistance to its first director, Robin Bird. I would like to express my thanks to members of the present editorial team for their encouragement and help in the production of this work, particularly to David Clark, Anthony Gosling and Jackie Friston. I am indebted to my wife, Cynthia, for her patience and support while this work was in preparation.

John J. Murray
December 2007

This has been a dark century for Christian literature. The history of evangelical publishing in the last ninety years is strewn with the graves of firms which expired amidst a dwindling market and with the spiritual wreckage of other firms, once evangelical but now the victims and servants of liberalism. With some notable exceptions, twentieth-century religious publishing has been more against the truth than for it, and just how low things have fallen can be judged by the fact that up until 1949 when John Calvin's Institutes *were reprinted by James Clarke and Co., there was not a well-known publishing firm in the land interested in printing Reformed books.*

IAIN MURRAY (February 1961)

Charles Haddon Spurgeon

1.

Losing the vision: 1900-1950

If we are to have a proper understanding of the change that took place in the history of the Christian church in the United Kingdom and in other parts of the world during the middle decades of the twentieth century, we need to take a brief look at the state of Christianity in the first half of that century.

The rise of liberalism in the nineteenth century

By the end of the nineteenth century it was clear that a wind of change was blowing through the Protestant churches of the United Kingdom. This was due to the spread of Higher Criticism in the theological colleges of the land. This teaching encouraged the study of biblical texts not only for their literary origins and history, but also for the meaning and intention of the human authors themselves. It had its origins in the 1860s in the universities of Germany, where it was the accepted practice for students from the UK who aspired to advancement in academic circles to do specialist studies. The change that came about in theological thought was justified in the name of progress and of biblical scholarship. Those scholars affected did not reject the Bible totally, but they believed that the new light and understanding given to them required that modifications should be made in the message of the church in order to win the approval of the majority. By doing this, they thought that the church would command greater influence in the world.

This proved to be a disastrous change and a significant turning point in church history. Some saw the danger signals and warned their contemporaries. Chief among them was the great Baptist preacher Charles Haddon Spurgeon (1834-92), who fought a rearguard action in what became known as 'the Downgrade Controversy'. He resigned from the Baptist Union over the liberal teaching that had infiltrated the denomination. Towards the end of his life he was regarded as 'the last of the Puritans'. In his address to the annual conference of the Pastor's College in 1889 he declared:

> What is being done today will affect the next centuries, unless the Lord should very speedily come... For my part, I am quite willing to be eaten of dogs for the next fifty years; but the more distant future will vindicate me.[1]

It is interesting to compare Spurgeon's prophetic words with those of one of the prominent liberal theologians, Dr Marcus Dods of the New College, Edinburgh. In a letter to a friend on 8 January 1902 he wrote:

> I wish I could live as a spectator through the next generation to see what they are going to make of things. There will be a grand turn up in matters theological. The churches won't know themselves fifty years hence. It is to be hoped some little rag of faith may be left when all's done. For my own part I am sometimes entirely under water and see no sky at all.[2]

Liberalism led to the dismantling of much of historic Christianity by the turn of the twentieth century. Whatever show of scholarship it may have presented, there is no doubt that liberalism was just disguised unbelief. It undermined belief in the supernatural, and presented the church with a God who was no longer regarded as transcendent. The essence of the true biblical faith, rediscovered at the time of the Protestant Reformation, was enshrined in the historic confessions of faith and catechisms of the Reformation and Puritan eras. Although some could not claim to call themselves 'Reformed' in the historic sense of that word, they would nevertheless hold to the biblical faith in what is known as the 'Calvinistic' or 'free grace' doctrines. B. B. Warfield was right to claim that 'the central fact of Calvinism is the vision of God' and 'its determining principle is zeal for the divine honour'.

It begins, it centres and it ends with the vision of God in his glory and it sets itself, before all things, to render God his rights in every sphere of life-activity... It is the vision of God and His Majesty, in a word, which lies at the foundation of the entirety of Calvinistic thinking.[3]

It is truly the echo of that Scripture which declares: 'For of him and through him and to him are all things to whom be glory for ever' (Romans 11:36).

If the Reformed faith is Christianity seen in terms of giving all the glory to God, then liberalism, in essence, is 'Christianity' harmonized with the religious aspirations of men and giving the glory to man. Liberalism made Christianity man-centred. It assumed the goodness of human nature and portrayed Christianity in terms of 'doing' rather than believing, of achieving rather than receiving. It looked chiefly to the human level and saw the business of religion mainly as the support of people. It was truth modified to give offence to none. The liberals surrendered doctrine in favour of 'life'.

The influence of liberalism in universities and colleges

The emergence of Christian Unions in the English universities was a feature of the last quarter of the nineteenth century. The first to be founded was the Cambridge Inter-Collegiate Christian Union (CICCU) in 1877. Among the factors that gave impetus to the rise of others were the missions of the American evangelist D. L. Moody in 1882 and the 'Cambridge Seven' in 1884. On 15 October 1889 a 'Missionary Convention for Young Men' took place in the Metropolitan Tabernacle, London, with C. H. Spurgeon in the chair.

> Over 1,500 students attended it with much enthusiasm. At the close of the convention one hundred and fifty-two London students signed the declaration that 'It is my earnest hope if God permit to engage in foreign missionary work.'[4]

Out of this grew the Student Volunteer Missionary Union (SVMU), inaugurated in 1892. The following year the British Colleges Christian Union was established and began to hold joint conferences with the SVMU. These groups were part of what soon came to be known as the Student Christian Movement (SCM).

During the early years of the twentieth century the influential elements in the SCM grew more committed to an open basis of belief that permitted all theological viewpoints, with the result that in 1910 the CICCU dissociated from the rest of the SCM on doctrinal grounds. By the outbreak of the First World War the great student movement known as SCM had become a very uncomfortable place for evangelicals to work in. The tragedy of war further heightened their sense of crisis. By the end of World War I the main emphases in the SCM were no longer the earlier biblical ones. Professor A. Rendle Short, commenting on the state of Christianity in English universities, believed that before 1914 'the situation was disquieting, almost calamitous, except at Cambridge, and at a few London medical schools… The real message of the gospel of forgiveness of sins in virtue of our Lord's atoning death had almost died out in the provincial universities.'[5]

As the century wore on, there were very few conservative evangelical scholars to be found teaching in the universities and colleges and such students were frequently subjected to ridicule by fellow students and often by their tutors. To quote Professor Short again: 'The idea has got abroad that men of learning, and especially the scientists, have made the Bible impossible of belief for anyone without a modern education.'[6] Few came out of their theological education unscathed. Dr T. R. Glover, writing in *The Times* in 1932, rejoiced in the change that had taken place and wrote: 'Today if you want a real old obscurantist college, you have to found one.'[7]

Effect of liberalism in the churches

The established denominations were going adrift in the direction of their leaders. The prevailing view was that no matter how much of the Bible was rejected by scholars, the essence of Christianity remained unaffected, After all, it was said, 'Christianity is a life not a doctrine.' This was the spirit that came to prevail in the churches. In 1907 a Congregational minister, R. J. Campbell, published a book entitled *The New Theology*. Influenced by the so-called 'new science' and especially by evolutionary theories, he expounded an almost pantheistic concept of God, denied the uniqueness of the incarnation and repudiated the miraculous. Many leaders in the church who held critical views of the Bible still spoke in the devotional language of the old gospel truths that they had learned in childhood. The people in the pews did not apprehend the dangers. Too many of them erred on the side of a false charity.

S. M. Houghton, writing of the Methodism in which he was reared in the 1920s, said,

> The church into which I was born was largely given over to 'modern thought' in its colleges and in its pulpits. Lord Tennyson, in his day, might sing of ringing in the true and ringing out the false, but the ringers of Methodism were 'ringing the changes' by abandoning the biblical doctrines to a large extent and welcoming doctrines 'which their fathers knew not'. Yet as a tyro [novice] I was convinced that Wesleyan Methodism was Christian to a high degree, in fact all that could be desired of a Christian church.[8]

During these years conservative evangelicals in the denominations became more unpopular with the established leaders and were increasingly isolated. As a result, like C. H. Spurgeon, they found it difficult to take effective action within their denominations. Their main recourse was to support one another in fellowships and societies that stood four square on the authority of Scripture. But in withdrawing from the contemporary religious scene, the danger for evangelicals was to live in a non-intellectual world of their own. They became wary of theology, partly because so many young evangelical students seemed to lose their distinctive beliefs when they studied at university or college.

Following the visit of D. L. Moody in the early 1870s the outlook of evangelicals in the UK was dominated by campaign-type evangelism and Arminianism. Nevertheless, the evangelicalism that prevailed throughout the first half of the twentieth century retained the essentials of the gospel. It believed that men's souls are lost, that conversion is an indispensable necessity, and that separation from the world and holiness of life should characterize the Christian. But increasingly there was less emphasis upon doctrine and less attention paid to historic Christianity. An appreciation of the place of church history was almost non-existent. The Reformers and the Puritans were practically forgotten. The vision of God in his glory was rapidly disappearing from view and thinking in the church became more and more man-centred.

Scarcity of evangelical literature

The decline in appreciation of the Reformed heritage was reflected in the Christian literary world. When we look back to the previous century and consider the influence that the writings of the Puritans had on C. H. Spurgeon and the manner in which he promoted them, it was clear that a sad change had set in. It was the discovery of a library that had been preserved for almost 200 years that introduced young Spurgeon to the riches of Puritan literature. In the manse adjoining the old Meeting House at Stambourne he found the minister's study — the window of which had been blocked up through the window-duty (a tax on windows in a house).

> In my time, it was a dark den — but *it contained books* and this made it a gold mine to me ... Here I first struck up acquaintance with the martyrs and especially with 'Old Bonner' who burned them; next with Bunyan and his 'Pilgrim'; and further with the great Masters of Scriptural theology, with whom no moderns are worthy to be named in the same day.[9]

The sermons and writings of Spurgeon showed just what an effect these discoveries had on him and what an influence he had in the republication and promotion of the works of the Puritans during his life.

In the early decades of the twentieth century the state of Christianity could be gauged by the decline of interest in the Christian classics, especially the Puritan writings, and by the type of literature that was becoming increasingly popular. At the time of the First World War Puritan books were often thrown out for salvage. It has been said that £12 a ton was the going price for unwanted books. Between the two World Wars demand for the older Christian books scarcely existed. John Stott could write:

> When I was an undergraduate at Cambridge University in the early 1940s (a vulnerable and immature evangelical believer, beleaguered by liberal theologians) there was no evangelical literature available to help me. In those days one had to ransack second-hand booksellers for volumes like A. H. Finn's *The Unity of the Pentateuch*, James Orr's *The Problem of the Old Testament*, R. W. Dale on *The Atonement* or works of the Princeton divines. But there was virtually no contemporary evangelical theology and IVP had not yet come into existence.

It was about this time that the writings of C. S. Lewis on the Christian faith began to fill a gap. In 1933 he had written *The Pilgrim's Regress,* which is partly autobiographical and an allegory about one route to the Christian faith. A publisher who liked it asked Lewis to write a book on suffering, which resulted in *The Problem of Pain.* It was admired by the BBC Director of Religious Broadcasting, who invited Lewis to give some radio talks. Lewis agreed that ordinary British people needed to hear what Christianity really is in language that they could understand. His aim was evangelistic and he gave a series of three talks, each of which was published in turn: *Broadcast Talks* (1942); *Christian Behaviour* (1943); and *Beyond Personality* (1944). These three were later put together and revised by Lewis to form one of his most famous books, *Mere Christianity* (1952).

Resistance to liberalism

The Protestant liberalism that prevailed for some forty years was given a setback by the social upheaval of the First World War and by the rise of neo-orthodoxy. The theological shift was led by Karl Barth, who chastised the liberals for making God after their own experiential image — God had become a liberal nine feet tall! Barth went back to the Bible and discovered that the Scripture is all about God in his own absolute 'Godness'. The new insights he had discovered were given to the world, particularly in his *Commentary on Romans,* published in 1918. Sadly Barth, although shifting the focus back to God, failed to reaffirm the truth of the absolute authority of the Bible as the Word of God. The resulting Barthianism, or neo-orthodoxy as it was called, was a false dawn that led many people further astray.

In the United States there was an early reaction to liberalism. A series of tracts for the times began to appear in 1909. Their publication was financed by two wealthy brothers called Lyman and Milton Stewart. There were sixty-five booklets in the series and millions of copies were sold. They were entitled *The Fundamentals* and covered such themes as the inspiration and authority of Scripture, the deity of Christ, his virgin birth and bodily resurrection, the Holy Spirit, sin, judgement, atonement, justification and regeneration. They were written in order for ministers of the gospel, missionaries, Sunday school superintendents etc., to have at their disposal articles which would be useful in affirming and reaffirming the fundamental truths of Christianity. The authors were drawn from North America and Britain and included such well-known evangelicals as B. B. Warfield, R. A. Torrey, A. T. Pierson, J. C. Ryle, Handley Moule and Campbell Morgan. However the Fundamentalist Movement was not entirely a continuation of historic evangelical Christianity. Many of the leaders adopted the premillennial and dispensationalist view of Scripture and this was often regarded by them as a fundamental article of the faith.

J. Gresham Machen, in 1932, at the home of W. J. Grier

What proved to be the more orthodox reaffirmation of the historic Christian faith came through the testimony to the truth by J. Gresham Machen. Trained at Princeton Theological Seminary, under B. B. Warfield, he did further studies in universities in Germany, and at Marburg was shaken in his faith for a time under the influence of the liberal theologian, Wilhelm Herrmann. Machen's testing in the German crucible proved to be the tempering of the steel in his character so that he would emerge later as a champion of orthodoxy. By 1925 he published his benchmark book entitled *Christianity and Liberalism,* in which he argued that Christianity and liberalism are two distinct religions. This led to a confrontation within Princeton Seminary and in the Presbyterian Church in the USA (PCUSA). In 1929 when the PCUSA reorganized Princeton to ensure a more inclusive theological spectrum, Machen and others withdrew and founded Westminster Theological Seminary at Philadelphia. The battle within the denomination continued and the crisis came to a head in 1935 when Machen was defrocked and the following year lost his appeal. He played the central role in the founding of a new denomination, named the Presbyterian Church of

America, then renamed the Orthodox Presbyterian Church in 1939, as a result of a law suit.

It was in the year 1929, which proved a watershed in the USA, that an initiative was taken in the United Kingdom to counteract liberalism and neo-orthodoxy. One of the few colleges not affected by liberalism was the Free Church of Scotland College in Edinburgh. Two of the professors from that faculty, Dr John R. Mackay and Dr Donald MacLean, launched the *Evangelical Quarterly* in January 1929. The journal was an attempt to articulate the historic Christian faith in the face of the threats that were arising, especially from neo-orthodoxy. They sought to rally Reformed men from around the world to this cause. The main contributors outside the UK were to come from Holland and North America.

In the first issue, the challenge of expounding the basic principles of the Reformed faith was given to Caspar Wistar Hodge of Princeton Theological Seminary, grandson of the great Charles Hodge. He gives a sober assessment of the situation:

Doubtless this Reformed Faith is suffering a decline in the theological world today. What has been termed 'Reformed spring-time in Germany' we cannot regard as the legitimate daughter of the classical Reformed Faith. In Scotland the names of William Cunningham and Thomas Crawford no longer exert the influence we wish they did. In America the influence of Charles Hodge, Robin Breckinridge, James Thornwell, Robert Dabney, William G. T. Shedd and Benjamin Warfield, seems largely to have vanished.[10]

Though in theological circles and in ecclesiastical courts the leaders of Reformed thought find scant recognition, wherever humble souls catch the vision of God in his glory and bow in humility and adoration before him, trusting for salvation only in his grace and power, there you have the essence of the Reformed Faith, and God in his providence may raise up a leader of religious thought who shall once again make the Reformed Faith a power in the theological world. If and when this happens we may confidently expect a true revival of religion in the Protestant world.

CASPAR WISTAR HODGE

E. J. Poole-Connor

2.

Recovering the vision: the forerunners

In the history of the work of redemption there are highs and lows, growth and dearth, revival and declension. Before times of reformation and revival God has frequently sent precursors of 'the coming dawn'. In the Scriptures we have the case of John the Baptist and in church history we have men like John Hus and John Wycliffe. Amid the darkness of the 1920s and 1930s there were flickers of light which can be viewed as the harbingers of a new day.

The year 1919 and the Inter-Varsity Fellowship

We saw in the previous chapter how the Student Christian Movement was influenced by the liberalism that spread in the churches toward the end of the nineteenth century. Then in the year 1919 a band of students sought to make 'a Luther-type stand' against it. Although a small remnant of fifteen students had kept Cambridge Inter-Collegiate Christian Union's light burning during the First World War, in the summer of 1919 Norman Grubb was told by leaders of the SCM that the atoning blood of Christ was not necessarily central in the beliefs of the movement. However, in the course of the CICCU summer camp at the Keswick Convention that year something happened that had a formative effect on student work. 'Those undergraduates who met for prayer in Mrs C. T. Studd's house at the 1919 Keswick Convention prayed until two in the morning. They affirmed "we had never before known such assurance in prayer".'[1] A sense of empowerment came over them and they went back to Cambridge to see some outstandingly gifted students converted and the membership rising from the 'entrenched' fifteen to fifty during that academic session.

A few months after the convention, one of them was praying in Trinity College, Cambridge, when the vision came to him of the future IVF. Norman Grubb wrote:

> I cannot remember the exact day but it was some time in the middle of the Michaelmas term 1919, that in my room in Trinity College, God gave me a clear vision of the IVF that was to be. I saw that not only must there be this witness in every university, but that God was going to do it. Probably the fact of Noel Palmer's prompt action in Oxford at the end of the 1914-18 war in getting to work to re-start an inter-collegiate Christian Union enabled God to open our eyes to this much better thing.[2]

Noel Palmer had been recovering from war wounds at Cambridge when Norman Grubb took him to hear a CICCU speaker, Barclay Buxton, and he was converted. He carried his enthusiasm for the gospel back to Oxford and soon meetings for Bible study and prayer were being held in many parts of the university.

Norman Grubb placed before the CICCU committee proposals for holding meetings in London for prayer for all the universities. The result was 'An Inter-Varsity Convention for all University Men' held in the Hall, 10 Drayton Park, London, from 8 to 11 December 1919. This was the first Inter-Varsity Conference. No report on this conference has been found and no minutes were kept.

The London Inter-Hospital Christian Union had functioned since 1912. From 1919 Christian Unions developed in the main colleges of London University and when the hospital CUs merged with these other CUs to become the London Inter-Faculty Christian Union (LIFCU) it set a pattern of what IVF was to become. Conferences in London were held in 1920, 1922, 1923 and 1924. The first residential conference was held at High Leigh, Hoddesdon, from 26 March to 1 April 1926, with eighty-two delegates from the unions present, and Bishop Taylor Smith and George Goodman among the speakers.

As more Christian Unions came into being, the need to visit the universities became apparent. In 1925 the conference executive committee asked Hugh R. Gough, the retiring CICCU President, if he would postpone entry to theological college and complete a full tour of the British universities. He agreed and so became the first full-time travelling secretary and gave timely impetus to the existing unions. At a meeting of the committee on 3 April 1928 proposals were put forward for the linking of the unions under the name of the 'Inter-Varsity Fellowship of Evangelical Christian Unions', a doctrinal basis was drawn up and a draft constitution was adopted.[3]

In the same year, following a plea from Norman Grubb about the opportunities presented in universities in Canada, Howard Guinness was appointed as an ambassador to promote evangelical witness in universities in North America. He extended his influence into English-speaking countries of the Commonwealth, which led eventually to the holding of international conferences prior to the Second World War and the launch in 1947 at Boston, New England, of the International Fellowship of Evangelical Students (IFES).

E. J. Poole-Connor and contending for the faith

A man whose life spanned the changes that were taking place in the church from the 1880s to the 1960s was Edward Joshua Poole-Connor. He was born into a Christian and staunchly Protestant home on 27 July 1872. As a child he was delicate and it was taken for granted that he would never reach manhood. His father was a deacon in Trinity Church, Hackney, London — a Calvinistic Independent Church, which had retained its orthodoxy.

He was converted early in life, and during his teens he taught a Sunday school class. He had opportunity to hear some of the great preachers of the day, and on one occasion, when Poole-Connor was ten years old, he was taken to worship at the Metropolitan Tabernacle. 'As he stood near one of the exits, Mr Spurgeon was escorted out to his carriage. The great man saw him, stopped, shook his hand, and with a few words left a lasting impression of extreme kindness and of a face aglow with the love of God.'[4] When Poole-Connor was thirteen his father fell ill and he had to leave school to help run the family business. At the age of fifteen he joined the membership of Trinity Church and expressed a desire to enter the ministry. He preached his trial sermon when he was eighteen and, after a year ministering in a small church in South Hackney, in 1893 he accepted a call to Aldershot Baptist Church, where he spent four happy years.

Following on from that, he ministered for two years in Borough Road Baptist Church, Elephant and Castle, London, and then in 1900 became minister of the Baptist church at Surbiton, Surrey. Contending with the modernism in the Baptist Union he resigned from there, following a ten-year fruitful ministry. After two years assisting at Lansdowne Hall, West Norwood, London, he was called in January 1913 to Talbot Tabernacle in Bayswater, London. This was a thriving Independent congregation and an offspring of the 1859 Revival. It was originally a large iron structure but was replaced in 1888 by a handsome stone building, dedicated by C. H. Spurgeon. Poole-Connor's expository preaching was much appreciated by the congregation.

With the marked increase in the influence of liberalism in the denominations there came into being more and more 'independent' congregations, including a number from the Baptist Union. When, in 1921, Poole-Connor was called to become full-time Deputation Secretary of the North Africa Mission he was brought face to face with the needs of these churches throughout the country. There seemed to be little fellowship or association between such assemblies. He sought to remedy the situation and in 1922 was instrumental in forming the 'Fellowship of Undenominational and Unattached Churches and Missions'. The movement increased and developed, and then changed its name to 'the Fellowship of Independent Evangelical Churches' (FIEC), which proved a rallying ground for many congregations from mixed denominations.

Poole-Connor continued to witness by tongue and pen for the defence of the faith. In 1933 he produced *The Apostasy of English Non-Conformity*, in which he dealt with the aftermath of the Downgrade Controversy and the baneful influence of the views of such men as Dr T. R. Glover and Dr A. S. Peake. His best-known literary work, *Evangelicalism in England*, was published in 1951, when he was seventy-nine, with a foreword by Dr Martyn Lloyd-Jones. In 1954 he was a leader, on behalf of the FIEC, in the formation of the British Evangelical Council, which was destined to come to greater prominence in English evangelicalism after 1966. The same year he was invited to become Editor of the *Bible League Quarterly*, which stood unequivocally for the verbal inerrancy of the Word of God. His significant contribution to the establishing of the Evangelical Library in London will be considered later.

It was a wonderful providence that E. J. Poole-Connor, after all his contendings for the faith, lived to see 'the beginning of a better day'. He saw in Dr Lloyd-Jones in particular a man with whom he could resonate. Two days after an Evangelical Alliance rally held on 18 June 1957 he wrote:

> Oh my dear Doctor — I heartily thank God, and thank you, for your address at the Alliance meeting on Tuesday last! You always manage to say the things that need to be said, but what nobody else will say... How my heart went out to your words about revival! There lies our hope.[5]

In the autumn of 1958, writing about 'the remarkable revival of interest in what may broadly be termed Puritan theological literature' and referring to the contributions of the Evangelical Library and the Banner of Truth Trust, Poole-Connor made a remarkable prophecy:

> It is our hope that this re-awakened interest in works that represent a warmer, a more reverential, and a more spiritually intelligent understanding of the Gospel, may herald a coming visitation of grace amongst the people of God, now so urgently needed. It is not infrequently one of the first evidences of a movement of God upon the soul that a man begins to turn to books that correspond to his new-born sense of need. May not this be now the case on a larger scale?[6]

A. W. Pink and *Studies in the Scriptures*

Another link between the Calvinism of C. H. Spurgeon, and the rediscovery of the doctrines of grace under the ministry of Dr D. M. Lloyd-Jones, was Arthur Walkington Pink. His life spanned the first half of the twentieth century. Converted in his home town of Nottingham in 1908 he went to the USA in

1910, and to the Moody Bible Institute. He remained there only two months before taking up a pastorate in Silverton, Colorado. When he left the institute he took with him one of their key study books, *The Scofield Bible.* He imbibed its Dispensationalist teaching and became deeply involved with the Fundamentalist Movement, and with some of its leaders, especially A. C. Gaebelein, who edited the well-known magazine, *Our Hope.*

A. W. Pink, 1910

After a few years Pink gradually came to question some of these 'popularly accepted beliefs'. The instrumental cause in this appears to have been the writings of the leaders of historic Christianity in former centuries. The first of the newly discovered authors to unsettle his thinking was Jonathan Edwards. Other authors of the same school arrested his attention and he went back afresh to the Bible. Pink had an experience in Christian literature reminiscent of the discovery of books made by the young C. H. Spurgeon in Stambourne. As he read the Christian classics, the more convinced he became that it was not only liberalism that was endangering the Christian faith but also fundamentalism, with its man-centred programmes for soul-winning.

In the providence of God the 'new' teaching of A. W. Pink caught the eye of I. C. Herendeen who owned a book depot at

Swengel, Pennsylvania. He went to visit Pink in 1917 and the two men discovered how they had both been led to a common mind with regard to the foremost weaknesses of contemporary Christianity. The outcome was a book from Pink's pen in June 1918 entitled *The Sovereignty of God,* one of the most influential publications to appear in the first half of the twentieth century. Herendeen had reservations over what he thought were elements of Hyper-Calvinism in it. In the foreword Pink writes:

> It would be foolish for us to expect that this work will meet with general approval. The trend of modern theology, if theology it can be called, is ever toward the deification of the creature rather than the glorification of the Creator.[7]

Pink became more and more acquainted with the writings of the Puritans. On 15 May 1919 he writes: 'Next week, DV, I shall complete Manton's 22 volumes, and then I expect to make a careful study of twelve large volumes by Thomas Goodwin.'[8] The doctrines of free grace and the experimental teaching of the Puritans brought a change to his preaching. Some former friends no longer used his services in preaching and it was difficult for him to find an appreciative audience. This led him to start, in 1922, a small magazine entitled *Studies in the Scriptures.* It pointed its readership back to an understanding of the gospel that had rarely been heard in England since the days of C. H. Spurgeon. This magazine, and the book titles later printed from the material contained in it, became a significant element in the recovery of the doctrines of grace, expository preaching and biblical living in the middle of the century. By the time of Pink's death in 1952, in virtual isolation in Stornoway, Isle of Lewis, *Studies in the Scriptures* was feeding the souls of several of the men who were to become leaders in that return to doctrinal Christianity.

Jay Green and the Sovereign Grace Book Club

As A. W. Pink was passing from the scene of time the fruit of his labours was already appearing. His friend, Mr I. C. Herendeen, had made a significant contribution to the recovery of Calvinistic teaching through his publishing programme. His successor at the Bible Truth Depot was Don Reiner. He began working with Herendeen in the early 1950s and then bought him out and re-named the publishing work Reiner Publications. At that time a new figure came on the publishing scene in the USA in the person of Jay Green. He was born in 1919 and converted at the age of thirty: 'I was suddenly made alive in Christ Jesus.' He came under the tutelage of a godly preacher who introduced him to the Puritans and he 'was accepted as a student by mail by A. W. Pink.'[9] His day job was as a salesman for Remington typewriters.

Jay Green was filled with a zeal to make known the writings of the old divines and promote their republication by subscription and mail order. In 1951 he made a start in drawing attention to the works of the Puritans by issuing a bimonthly magazine, *The Way, the Truth and the Life*, edited by himself. It was in 'late 1954' that the venture of reprinting the books of the old divines began, and the first to appear were *Prayer* by John Bunyan and *Keeping the Heart* by John Flavel. By 1959 he was working part time for Remington and devoting sixty hours a week to the publishing.

In October 1956 this reprint work that was taking place in the USA was drawn to the attention of readers of *The Banner of Truth*, a magazine that had been launched with a similar aim in Oxford, England, in 1955:

> The work Mr Green has begun is desperately needed. It has already in the USA been greatly blessed by God. The work which began without any financial capital, depended on the co-operation and support of believers. The manner in which the difficulties which faced such a project have

been overcome demonstrates how a few united men acting together can be instruments of the power of God... The organization of the Sovereign Grace Book Club in Britain Mr Green has entrusted to us. Mr Thomas Watson B.A., 48 Thorncliffe Road, Oxford, England is taking charge of this work.

The Editor of *The Banner of Truth* felt he had to add to the note:

Lastly, we ought to state that the Sovereign Grace Book Club has no connection with the organization of a similar name which exists in Britain.[10]

The organization referred to by the Editor was the Sovereign Grace Union. It had been formed as the Sovereign Grace Mission in 1875 and was reconstituted under the existing title in 1914 'for the proclamation and defence of Doctrines of Free and Sovereign Grace'. Regular meetings were held and books and pamphlets were issued. By the 1950s the leadership of the SGU had passed into the hands of those with a tendency toward Hyper-Calvinism.[11] Their literature found a ready market in some of the Strict and Particular Baptist Church circles. As the more historic Calvinism was recovered in the 1950s it influenced some of the men connected with these churches and out of them emerged leaders such as John Doggett and Robert Oliver, who were to play a significant part in the rediscovery of the vision.

Ernie Reisinger and the origins in Carlisle, USA

It is also important to notice the influence that I. C. Herendeen had on the start of the literature work at Carlisle, Pennsylvania,

USA. Ernie Reisinger, a businessman and a member of a Presbyterian church in Carlisle, had been converted and began to witness for Christ with some success. Some who were relishing the new-found Calvinistic truths prevailed on Ernie to join them in forming a church that would be loyal to the Word of God. This led to the founding, in 1951, of an assembly known as 'Grace Chapel'. Walter Chantry says,

Ernie Reisinger

> The spiritual energy of this fledgling group of young Christians was exciting. There was warm-hearted discipline in prayer, Bible study and evangelism. There was a deep hunger to learn the truth and lead a holy life.[12]

None of the men in the fellowship, including Ernie, had a well-informed understanding of doctrine. Ernie's brother John was at this time pastor of a church in Lewisburg, Pennsylvania. In that congregation was I. C. Herendeen of the Bible Truth Depot. Through persistent effort Herendeen persuaded John Reisinger of the truth of the doctrines of grace. Then Herendeen and John began to give books to the leaders of the recently formed Grace Chapel in Carlisle.

Ernie Reisinger, after initial resistance to the new teaching, had his eyes opened to the wonder of the sovereign grace of God in the gospel. His zeal to spread the newly discovered Reformed doctrine was unsurpassed. He led the way in working through

Grace Baptist Church, Carlisle, as it is now

the implications of the new teaching and by 1956 'Grace Chapel' had become Grace Baptist Church, subscribing to the *London Confession of Faith of 1689*. Ernie was tireless in evangelistic labours, writing letters and giving out books, especially to students and ministers. His book ministry led to the establishing of a book table at Grace Baptist Church and in the early 1960s the literature ministry took off. This gave birth to Puritan Publications Inc., which in the 1960s was selling more Banner of Truth titles than any other agent in the USA. Later in that decade Ernie Reisinger was to become the first American trustee of the Banner of Truth Trust. But we are going ahead of our story.[13]

W. J. Grier and the Evangelical Bookshop, Belfast

In the 1930s and 1940s the best Reformed books were being published in the USA. The main source of supply of these books in the United Kingdom was the Evangelical Bookshop in

Belfast. This work was established through the Rev. William J. Grier (1902-1983). 'Jim' Grier, as he was affectionately known, was converted on 24 October 1922 while a student at Queen's University, Belfast. He went on to study for two years (1923-25) at Princeton Theological Seminary in the USA. These two years made a profound impression on his life. He sat under the teaching of Caspar Wistar Hodge and J. Gresham Machen and learned to love the writings of the earlier Princeton men, like Charles Hodge and B. B. Warfield.

> These men both the living and the dead, established him in the Calvinism which has its source in the vision of God and his majesty. At Princeton he learned that passion for men's souls and zeal for the purity of the faith belong together.[14]

That zeal for the purity of the faith was soon put to the test. In the final year of his training at the Theological College of the Irish Presbyterian Church he had to listen to Professor J. E. Davey denying the divinity of Christ. Charges were brought against this professor by the Rev. James Hunter, and Mr Grier became a witness in the subsequent trial.[15] The professor was exonerated by the General Assembly and this resulted in a secession from the church, led by Mr Hunter and assisted by Mr Grier, and the formation of the Irish Evangelical Church (later known as the Evangelical Presbyterian Church). A bookshop had been started in the spring of 1926 under the auspices of the Presbyterian Bible Standards League — an organization set up to combat the false teaching. The initial stock consisted of Bibles, tracts and controversial pamphlets. They were displayed on a trestle table in the front room of a house. In October 1926 W. J. Grier became manager, partly to give him a job where he could not be unduly influenced by the church authorities, as he was a witness against the professor.

Rev. W. J. Grier

In October 1927, when the secession took place, the shop with its overdraft was offered to the PBSL members who stayed in the Irish Presbyterian Church. They refused the offer, which was then made to the seceders and they accepted it. The shop thus became the outlet and offices of the Irish Evangelical Church. Rev. James Hunter, his brother-in-law, Dr John Gillespie, and Mr John Patterson funded the operation and later became trustees. The premises at 15 College Square East, Belfast, were rented until 1944 when they were bought and a shop front put in. Rev. Grier worked in the mornings in the shop and performed his ministerial duties in the afternoons and evenings. His colleague from 1928, Mr S. G. Shanks, succeeded him as manager in the late 1940s, but Mr Grier continued as secretary to the trustees and as superintendent of the shop until the 1970s, particularly responsible for orders from the American publishers. The main publicity for the books came through the magazine, edited by Mr Grier, *The Irish Evangelical,* in which he vigorously advocated the importance of Reformed literature. In 1974 his son John returned from London to take over as manager of the bookshop and has continued in that work to the present time. John recalls the early days:

> As the Sabbath School Society (the PCI shop) had refused to import orthodox books by authors like J. Gresham Machen from the USA, W. J. Grier developed a major ministry of importing conservative books from US publishers like Wm B. Eerdmans. Later the shop served as distributor for them and a whole succession of firms: Presbyterian and Reformed Publishing, Baker Book House, Zondervan, Great Commission Publications. The vision was clearly to provide an orthodox conservative evangelical alternative to the liberal theology then dominant in the mainline churches. Following difficulties within the Irish Evangelical Church with premillennial dispensationalists in the early 1930s, a further emphasis on promoting more Biblical views of the Second Coming became essential.
>
> The shop right from PBSL days had always propagated the doctrines of the *Westminster Confession of Faith* and *Catechisms,* but its strong Calvinistic position came into greater prominence as the years passed. Evangelical bookshops and strongly committed Reformed publishers were few and far between in the UK in the 1930–1955 period. The effectiveness of the shop peaked in and immediately after the War years when it had a unique ministry in providing books by mail order to customers all over the British Isles. There were restrictions on import of supplies not vital to the War effort. W. J. Grier felt that his excessively optimistic ordering in the 1930s had providentially built up the large stock needed when supplies from the USA dried up in the War years.[16]

Other influences

As we have seen, Reformed books were being imported from the USA because there were few publishers producing such books at that time in the UK. James Clarke and Co., which had been founded in 1859 in Fleet Street mainly as a magazine publisher, became exclusively a book publishing company. They were persuaded, through the influence of Dr D. M. Lloyd-Jones, to publish the Beveridge edition of the *Institutes of the Christian Religion* by John Calvin in 1949, and a reprint of *Holiness* by J. C. Ryle (with a foreword by the Doctor) in 1952; and then undertook work on the seven-volume *Expository Thoughts on the Gospels* by J. C. Ryle in the years 1954 to 1958. Others became involved in the business of importing and selling Reformed titles from the US — notably Norman A. MacMillan in Doncaster and later Dr Jack Milner, who took on the Craig Press Agency in the UK.

Prior to the 1950s there were not many magazines promoting the free grace doctrines in the UK. One that came to the fore in January 1955 was *The Free Grace Record*. It was a small Strict Baptist quarterly but, under the editorship of John Doggett (1917-2006), it became an agent in the recovery of the Reformed faith in England.[17] Before Mr Doggett took over, the magazine circulated among a group of churches that had become introverted but his editorials challenged his readers to think biblically instead of traditionally. Its early contributors included Dr J. I. Packer and Professor F. F. Bruce. It appeared at a significant time of change and a welcome was given in its pages to the appearance of *The Banner of Truth* and the book publishing programme. A significant development arising from correspondence in *The Free Grace Record* was the republication of the *Baptist 1689 Confession of Faith* by John Doggett and two friends in 1959. The confession gained widespread acceptance and became the confession of the emerging Reformed Baptist churches in the 1960s.

R. B. Jones and others derived much of their inspiration from nineteenth-century Keswick teaching and the apologetic spirit of current American fundamentalism. Dr Lloyd-Jones was to reopen deeper wells and a return to a robust Biblical heritage — to the Reformers, the Puritans, the Calvinistic Methodist Fathers, to Spurgeon and to the Princeton Presbyterians.

GERAINT FIELDER

Without name or distinct organisation, a new tide of opinion was rising which, in its understanding of the situation, differed widely from the crusade ethos. The visible origins of this influence can be traced to such agencies as the Inter-Varsity Fellowship (with its books and student conferences), the annual Puritan Conference, the Evangelical Library, and publishers who had begun to reprint long-forgotten authors in the older evangelical and Reformed tradition. From small beginnings, with the reissue of works by John Calvin and J. C. Ryle, a near flood of books in the older tradition was to be found in Christian bookshops by the 1960s. These agencies were separate streams which overlapped with one another in their common influence. The name of only one man appeared in connection with them all and it was that of Martyn Lloyd-Jones.

IAIN MURRAY

Dr David Martyn Lloyd-Jones

3.

David Martyn Lloyd-Jones:
the recovery of the vision

i. The preparation of the man

As we have looked at the men and movements that preserved a testimony to the doctrines of free grace during the first half of the century, we now turn to consider the individuals who recaptured the vision and were used of God to bring about its recovery.

The words of Caspar Wistar Hodge in concluding his essay in the *Evangelical Quarterly,* January 1929, were to prove prophetic:

> Though in theological circles and in ecclesiastical courts the leaders of Reformed thought find scant recognition, wherever humble souls catch the vision of God in his glory and bow in humility and adoration before him, trusting for salvation only in his grace and power, there you have the essence of the Reformed Faith, and God in his providence may raise up a leader of religious thought who shall once again make the Reformed Faith a power in the theological world. If and when this happens we may confidently expect a true revival of religion in the Protestant world.[1]

We can gather from a study of church history that there is very often one individual raised up above others to forward a work of God. In the twentieth century that leader was undoubtedly Dr David Martyn Lloyd-Jones. During the 1940s and the early 1950s in England he stood almost alone as a champion of the true biblical faith. It was in the mid 1950s that the change first began to be observed. Looking back, it is clear that quite a number of men who were later associated with the Reformed recovery can trace their conversion, or their discovery of the doctrines of grace, to that time.

The Evangelical Library had opened its doors in London on 15 January 1945. The Puritan Conference began in the December of 1950. The writings of John Calvin and J. C. Ryle were being reprinted by James Clarke at the instigation of Dr Lloyd-Jones. Sovereign Grace Book Club in the USA began issuing Puritan classics in late 1954. The first issue of the *Banner of Truth* magazine appeared in September 1955. It is not surprising, then, that when addressing the Annual Meeting of the Evangelical Library in December 1955, Dr Lloyd-Jones could say:

> I feel that we are witnessing a true revival of interest in the Puritans, and a number of young men are studying their literature constantly. There is held annually a Puritan Conference which is attended by some sixty people, and this library has played a very central part in it.[2]

In the following year Dr Lloyd-Jones visited the United States and in December 1956 he reported back on the changes he found there:

> Among the leaders in evangelical work, and especially among the students I did find something which really did amaze me. After a meeting a number of young men came forward to speak with me and every single one talked to

me about Puritan literature and asked whether there was a possibility of getting Puritan books from this country. It is true of increasing numbers of them; they like us are turning to the Puritans, and for the same reason. We are all tired of the typical periodicals and books and are not being helped by the literature of today. They felt that they wanted something solid for their souls.[3]

Dr Lloyd-Jones, Geoffrey Williams and Friends of EL, 1956

Introduction to Calvinistic Methodism

David Martyn Lloyd-Jones was born on 20 December 1899 in Cardiff, where his father was a shopkeeper. When he was five years old the family moved to Llangeitho, the scene of the ministry of the famous Welsh preacher, Daniel Rowland. At the age of ten, young Martyn survived a fire in the family store and home, making his escape by a ladder being put to an upstairs window — an experience not dissimilar to that of the young

John Wesley. The first impressions made on the life of the young lad came at the meetings of the Summer Association of the Calvinistic Methodists, which were held at Llangeitho in 1913, to commemorate the bicentenary of Daniel Rowland's birth. He later recalled:

> That Association had a deep effect upon me, and possibly the most important thing it did was to create in me an interest in the Calvinistic Methodist Fathers which has lasted until today.[4]

Just a few weeks after that experience, as he stood in the playground at Tregaron School at the end of the summer term, his history master, S. M. Powell, thrust something into his pocket with the abrupt instruction, 'Read that'. It was a penny booklet on the ministry of Howell Harris, one of the foremost figures in the eighteenth-century revival in Wales. This was his first reading in the history of Calvinistic Methodism — a history from which he was later to gain a distinct view of the majesty and power of God.

In 1914 his father, Henry Lloyd-Jones, went to London to find work and bought a small dairy business in the Westminster area. After settling in the capital the family attended the Welsh Calvinistic Methodist Church at Charing Cross. Martyn was educated at Marylebone Grammar School. When he was sixteen he began to study medicine at St Bartholomew's Hospital (Bart's). He graduated MRCS and LRCP in July 1921 and MB and BS in October of that year, with distinction in medicine. His abilities were recognized by Sir Thomas Horder, the King's physician, who invited him to become his assistant.

It was when he was in his early twenties that a spiritual change occurred. Recalling that time he said,

> For many years I thought I was a Christian when in fact I was not. It was only later I came to see that I had never

been a Christian and became one. But I was a member of a church and attended my church and its services regularly.[5]

Eternal realities faced him through the deaths, first of his brother and then of his father. He also began to discern in practising medicine that the real malady lay not in men's bodies but in their minds and hearts. He also discovered that he himself was no different from the patients he was treating:

> God brought me to see that the real cause of all my troubles and ills and that of all men, was an evil nature which hated God and loved sin. My trouble was not only that I did things that were wrong, but that I myself was wrong at the very centre of my being.[6]

He could testify, having drunk at the fountain head of divine love: 'I am a Christian solely and entirely because of the grace of God and not because of anything I have thought or said or done.'

Discovering the English Puritans

It was about that time that he discovered the writings of the English Puritans. Speaking at the 1971 Puritan Conference on 'Puritanism and Its Origins' he said,

> My real interest arose in 1925 when, in a way I need not explain now, I happened to read a new biography of Richard Baxter which had just appeared. I had read a review of it in the then *British Weekly* and was so attracted that I bought it. From that time a true and living interest in the Puritans and their works has gripped me, and I am free to confess that my whole ministry has been governed by this.[7]

His 'discovery' of Baxter was followed by other seventeenth-century acquisitions purchased in second-hand bookshops in London. Presents from friends for his wedding included a second-hand set of the *Works of John Owen*. In the course of time Owen was to be preferred to Baxter.

It is a remarkable fact that some who became ministers of the gospel knew a sense of that calling given to them before they were converted. Such was the case with Dr Lloyd-Jones. Now he found himself in the throes of a struggle as to whether or not it was right to abandon medicine. By June 1926 the struggle was over: 'It was God's hand that laid hold of me and drew me out and separated me to this work.'

He believed that he was not meant to pursue his denomination's course of theological education. Instead he became concerned with the need for evangelistic work among poorer, working-class people in Wales. After a talk with his minister he was directed to the home-mission agency of the Presbyterian Church of Wales (Calvinistic Methodist Church) known as 'The Forward Movement', which represented an attempt to reverse the dwindling influence of the denomination upon the unchurched. He was later to explain that his father's radical views and his concern for the poor and underprivileged had had a profound effect upon him.[8]

In February 1927 he became the minister of Bethlehem Forward Movement Mission Hall in Sandfields, a locality in the South Wales town of Aberavon.

In an interview with Dr Carl Henry near the end of his life he was to say:

> I deliberately went to South Wales, to a small mission centre of 93 members, to do pioneer work. The mission under the Welsh Presbyterian Church, was in both a mining district and a centre of steel and tinplate works. Many of the people were dock labourers.

In that working-class community, through his Spirit-anointed labours, God called and redeemed many remarkable trophies of grace. In 1930 seventy souls were added to the congregation and the following year a further 128. 'In my eleven and a half years the church grew to 530 members and the attendance ran to about 850.'[9]

An annexe had to be built alongside the church building, enabling the overflowing numbers to follow the services through the open windows of the chapel.

Discovering the writings of Edwards and Warfield

It was during his ministry in Sandfields that he became acquainted with some new authors. He was challenged at the close of a service in Bridgend by a minister who commented provocatively: 'I cannot make up my mind what you are. I cannot decide whether you are a Hyper-Calvinist or a Quaker.' On being asked why the comment was being made, he was told: 'You talk of God's actions and God's sovereignty like a Hyper-Calvinist and of spiritual experience like a Quaker, but the Cross and the work of Christ have very little place in your preaching.' Assuring him that he was not a Hyper-Calvinist, the Doctor's response was to ask the Rev. Vernon Lewis, when he called the following Monday morning, what he could recommend him to read on the atonement. He was referred to the works of P. T. Forsyth, R. W. Dale's *The Atonement,* and J. Denney's *The Death of Christ* — such was the dearth of truly evangelical literature at the time.[10] These writings gave a new tincture to the Doctor's preaching.

While he was still living in London, Lloyd-Jones had asked a minister of the Welsh Presbyterian Church for titles that would help him to prepare for the ministry. One recommendation he received was *Protestant Thought Before Kant* by A. C. Mcgiffert.

While reading it he came across the name of Jonathan Edwards for the first time. This sent him on a search:

> After much searching I at length called at John Evans' bookshop in Cardiff in 1929, having time available as I waited for a train. There down on my knees in my overcoat in a corner of the shop I found the two volume 1834 edition of Edwards which I bought for five shillings. I devoured these volumes and literally just read and read them. It is certainly true they helped me more than anything else.[11]

He was later to say, 'I was like the man in our Lord's parable who found a pearl of great price. Their influence upon me I cannot put into words.'

In 1932 'Dr Martyn', as he was known in the church at Sandfields, went on a visit to Canada. During the nine-week stay there, his accommodation was located opposite the Knox Seminary, a leading Presbyterian theological school. Granted permission to use the facilities of its library he discovered, on his first entrance to the building, the recently published *Works of B. B. Warfield* standing on the shelves reserved for new acquisitions. His feelings at that moment, he was later to write, were like those of 'stout Cortez', as described by Keats, when he first saw the Pacific. To Warfield more than to anyone else he was to attribute a development in his thought and ministry which occurred at this period. He said, 'Such was Warfield's own knowledge and experience of the truth, and of God in Christ through the Holy Spirit that more than most writers he gives us a profound impression of the glory and wonder of the salvation we enjoy.' Warfield gave him a new insight into the necessity for doctrinal preaching and for the defence of the truth from the attacks of unbelieving scholarship. 'He not only asserted the Reformed Faith; he at the same time demonstrated its superiority over all other systems or partial systems.'[12]

It was late in 1935 that Dr Lloyd-Jones received an invitation from Dr Campbell Morgan to preach at Westminster Chapel, Buckingham Gate, London. This he fulfilled on 29 December 1935 and preached on the text John 6:66-68.[13] After his eleven years of intensive work in Sandfields, it was suggested that the denomination should appoint the Doctor to the staff of the Theological College of the Presbyterian Church of Wales at Bala. Some of the liberal religious leaders were prepared to resist this. At the time that the Doctor was inclined towards accepting the Bala vacancy, the news reached the ears of Dr Campbell Morgan. He took the opportunity to invite the Doctor for the interim period to come and alternate preaching services with him at Westminster Chapel.

Within six weeks he received a unanimous call to serve as associate pastor. At first he refused to commit himself, still waiting for a firm invitation to the college at Bala. The request never came and in the end the Doctor accepted the invitation to become associate minister at Westminster Chapel. In a tribute to the Doctor in the special Martyn Lloyd-Jones memorial issue of the Evangelical Movement of Wales magazine in 1981 Rev. Elwyn Davies said,

> In the hindsight of close on half a century we now know that that step, which to some might seem so regrettable at the time, proved to be possibly the most far-reaching and consequential development this century in the history of the evangelical cause in Britain, if not throughout the world.[14]

A link with A. W. Pink

An incident that took place in 1949 illustrates one of the many providential links we discover between the men that were used by God in the recovery of the Reformed vision. Dr Lloyd-Jones was so unwell with persistent catarrh and other symptoms of overwork, that he had to cancel a visit to the USA and went instead to his beloved Wales on holiday. He experienced a bout of depression together with an onslaught from the devil. It gave him a discovery of himself and of the pride of the human heart.

While seeking a cure he went to stay at a nursing home near Bristol. During his time there, the inner tempest continued. He had with him an issue of A. W. Pink's magazine, *Studies in the Scriptures.* Then one morning he awoke soon after six o'clock, in a complete agony of soul and even feeling a sense of evil in the room. As he started dressing, his eye caught just the word 'glory' in an article by Pink. Instantly, 'like a blaze of light', he felt the very glory of God surround him. Every doubt and fear was silenced. The love of God was 'shed abroad' in his heart. He was brought into a state of ecstasy and joy which remained with him for several days.[15]

That experience did much to shape the ministry of Dr Lloyd-Jones. He came to know himself and also the wiles of the devil. The hallmarks of a true experience of God are in his own words 'a sense of awe, and accompanying it a sense of unworthiness'. He came to see more deeply than ever before that the final explanation of the state of the church in his day was due to a defective sense of sin. There was a further change in his preaching. He increasingly saw that truth is to be preached in a manner which affects the heart and the conscience of the individual. He also urged the truth on his hearers that fellowship with God is more than doctrinal orthodoxy. Therefore love to God — a love which wholly possesses us — is the supreme need of the preacher.

It was given him in the post-war years to see the quality of evangelical teaching in England and change for the better through his own weaving back into it the binding thread of Reformed theology — a thread which had snapped after Spurgeon was defeated in the Downgrade controversy, and Keswick teaching swamped Anglican Calvinism, and liberalism and the social gospel captured the pulpits of Wales. Ultimately responsible for this ministry having the happy impact was Douglas Johnson, first General Secretary of the Inter-Varsity Fellowship, who both drew the Doctor into student work, where he could shape the outlook of the rising generation of evangelical leaders, and also persuaded him to found his influential ministers' fraternal, the Westminster Fellowship, which in fact made him bishop to literally hundreds of clergy in all denominations.

JAMES I. PACKER

Dr Martyn Lloyd-Jones

4.

David Martyn Lloyd-Jones: the recovery of the vision

ii. The multiplying of his influence

Following the outbreak of the Second World War, in September 1939, the number in the congregation at Westminster Chapel reduced to about 300 people. The services were held with blacked-out windows and the evening service was moved to mid-afternoon. Recalling those days the Doctor said,

> In a flying bomb attack a bomb dropped just across the road in June 1944 and blew off half the chapel roof, so that for 14 weeks we met in a borrowed hall with about 150 people. Only 100 to 200 were left of Campbell Morgan's great congregation. Campbell Morgan retired in 1943 and died in 1945.[1]

After the difficulties and discouragements of the war years, the congregation at Westminster Chapel began to grow. In a letter to Dr Philip E. Hughes on 17 April 1946, the Doctor said,

> Our congregations have been steadily increasing since the end of the war and we are having congregations both morning and evening of about 850 to 900 people. We are also seeing occasional conversions.[2]

Interior view of Westminster Chapel

By 1948 the numbers had increased to 1,300 to 1,400 and the first gallery of the church building had to be opened. The Friday evening 'Discussion Classes' had grown in numbers and during the years 1953-55 the meeting took the form of expositions of Christian doctrine. This was followed by the Doctor's exposition of the Epistle to the Romans, which he began in October 1957 and continued until March 1968. The chapel became a centre for true biblical preaching and many were brought to faith and established in the doctrines of free grace.

The ministry of Dr Lloyd-Jones and Westminster Chapel became a stimulus and an inspiration to many related agencies. Chief among them were the Evangelical Library, the Puritan Conference and the Banner of Truth Trust, all of which will be dealt with in subsequent chapters; but three significant strands of the Doctor's influence need to be interwoven into the picture at this stage: the Inter-Varsity Fellowship; the Evangelical Movement of Wales; and the Westminster Fellowship.

Inter-Varsity Fellowship: 'The Theologian of the IVF'

One area which greatly benefited from the influence of Dr Lloyd-Jones was the Christian student world. We have already seen how the Inter-Varsity Fellowship was formed in 1928. Four years later Dr Douglas Johnson, a medical graduate, became the first secretary employed, part time, by IVF. He was paid the princely sum of £87.10s, and a one-room office in Russell Square, London, was hired for £1 a week. Dr Johnson was to emerge as one of the most significant figures, not only in student work but also, in partnership with Dr Lloyd-Jones, in the recovery of Reformed evangelicalism in the UK.

Dr Gaius Davies, speaking at the memorial service for the Doctor in 1981, said,

> It is my belief that the close association between two medical men who had left the prospects of glittering prizes for the work of God's kingdom will feature largely in a true and proper account of Christian work in the middle of the 20th century.[3]

Johnson heard Lloyd-Jones for the first time at the Annual Meeting of the China Inland Mission in May 1934. He and other leaders of the IVF were impressed by what they heard and were determined to get the Doctor to speak at their Annual Conference in 1935. Johnson went all the way to Aberystwyth, where the Lloyd-Jones family were on holiday, to persuade him to speak. That long journey was not in vain, for Lloyd-Jones agreed to give one address at the next conference. However, his impressions of that IVF Conference were not favourable. He felt there was a lack of seriousness, and found that speakers and hearers had little interest in the literature that meant so much to him. Their sense of church history seemed to be non-existent and theology of any kind was viewed with suspicion.

From then on, it was theological leadership above everything else that the Doctor was to give to the IVF, both in public and in private. In his own words, 'I became the theologian of the IVF.' He made outstanding contributions in addressing the various conferences of the IVF and the Theological Students' Fellowship, which had been formed in 1933. This leadership was seen in particular at a private conference to plan for the future, held at Kingham Hill School, near Oxford, from 7-10 July 1941. The stated object of this conference was 'The revival of evangelical theology'. The Doctor spoke on 'The causes of present weakness'. From notes taken at the time by Douglas Johnson we have a clear picture of the insight the Doctor had to the contemporary evangelical scene and his grasp of the general principles required for the recovery of the church. The Kingham conference also highlighted the need to raise the level of evangelical scholarship for conservative works.

Reference has been made already to the dearth of evangelical literature at the right level for students. Sound scholarly works on the interpretation and exposition of the Bible were rare. In mission work among students IVF was greatly disadvantaged by lack of books to establish converts in biblical doctrine. During the run-up to one university mission, Jim Broomhall called to see Dr Johnson about this and said, 'Look if we get any conversions, how can we instruct them in the faith? We need something to establish people in Biblical doctrine.'[4] In 1936 Ronald Inchley, a recently qualified graduate with no publishing experience, was appointed as Literature Secretary at a salary of £180 per annum. The first substantial publication from Inter-Varsity was *In Understanding be Men* by T. C. Hammond (1936), which became a bestseller. This was followed by *Search the Scriptures* (1934-37) by G. T. Manley and H. W. Oldham, subsequently revised and altered, and *Why Believe* by Rendle Short (1938). These books became the basic diet for Christian students for a decade.

At first, resources for publishing were limited and distribution was poor. Doubts were expressed about its continuance and, with the outbreak of war, the secretary had to seek other employment. In 1945 Mr Inchley returned and the work began to progress. In 1947 there was the publication of *The New Bible Handbook*, edited by G. T. Manley, which sold out in a matter of weeks. The production of the *New Bible Commentary* in 1953 was a major step forward for the publishing arm of IVF, resulting in a profit for that year of £11,000. This was followed in 1956 by the launching of the Tyndale Commentary series under the editorship of Professor R. V. G. Tasker, whose 'life was revolutionised' by an address by the Doctor in King's College, London, in 1947.[5] The first major work from the ministry of Dr Lloyd-Jones, *The Sermon on the Mount,* appeared in two volumes in 1959-60.

In the late 1940s the Doctor, according to his biographer, 'seemed to be almost constantly engaged in the work of Inter-Varsity Fellowship, chairing committee or public meetings, preaching for the various Evangelical Unions at the Universities, speaking annually at conferences of the Theological Students' Fellowship or addressing meetings of graduates'. On top of that, he became involved in international gatherings. He was one of the founding members of the International Fellowship of Evangelical Students. Its predecessor was the International Conference of Evangelical Students which began in 1934. Lloyd-Jones had the distinction of addressing 900 or more students who gathered at Cambridge University for the 1939 conference. It was April 1946 before they met again and on this occasion there were delegates present from the USA, Canada and Australia. The Doctor was one of three British delegates. At this conference a new vision for the world was kindled and delegates were united in the need for a worldwide body — the International Fellowship of Evangelical Students.

A gathering was planned for Boston, USA, in August 1947 for the official formation of the IFES. Twenty-five delegates met in Harvard University, with Lloyd-Jones presiding over the assembly.

> With consummate skill and unimaginable patience, Dr Lloyd-Jones chaired this Conference until a constitution was hammered out and an international movement was formed.

That assessment was by Dr Stacey Woods, who became the first General Secretary of the IFES and was to work very closely with Dr Lloyd-Jones. He paid this tribute to the Doctor:

> During the first ten years of the International Fellowship of Evangelical Students, Dr Martyn Lloyd-Jones put his stamp upon the movement. He gave us backbone, conviction, a refusal to compromise, a willingness to stand alone against the World Council of Churches and the World Student Christian Federation if necessary.[6]

The Evangelical Movement of Wales: 'The people of the magazine'

When Dr Lloyd-Jones went to London in 1938 it could have been said, 'Wales's loss was surely England's gain.' That was only partly true, because the Doctor probably exercised a greater influence on Wales from his vantage point in London than if he had been head of the denomination's theological college in Bala. While the Doctor's visits to Wales before 1945 were mainly to address large congregations, his ministry after that date took a new form. He assumed the role of friend and adviser to a body of young students who were to be, under God, the instruments in recovering the evangelical faith in the churches of Wales.

Evangelical student witness in Wales was first begun at University College, Cardiff, by the bold initiative of David John Thomas. At first he was unaware of what was happening at other UK universities but on making contact with Dr Rendle Short he was told what had happened in Cambridge, Oxford and London, with students breaking away from the SCM — and 'the remarkable way in which these bodies had been formed simultaneously, without any human organisation'. 'Cardiff Students' Evangelical Union' was constituted on 2 February 1923.[7] The work progressed and in 1927 Dr Lloyd-Jones, newly inducted minister at Sandfields, was the speaker there. Cardiff Union was followed by ones at Aberystwyth in 1928 and at Swansea in 1930.

It appears that the 1930s were a time of struggle for the evangelical unions. A change came in the 1940s when a movement of God among students was to reach out to touch the life of the congregations. 'One of the spearheads of the change was a series of student campaigns that began the very year that things began to look up at Cardiff, in 1940.'[8] The campaign in Cardiff was followed by others in the Rhondda (1941), Carmarthen (1944) and Llanelli (1945). Remarkable numbers attended and numerous conversions took place. At Llanelli in 1945, where Glyn Owen was one of the speakers, two young students were converted on the Sunday night before the mission began. They were John B. E. Thomas and Hugh Morgan, both of whom were destined to become leading figures in the Evangelical Movement of Wales. On the way home from the mission on the Monday night they witnessed to two girls, Eluned Rees and Mari Williams. The girls were converted at the Tuesday night meeting and later became their respective wives.

It was not long before things began to happen in North Wales. J. Elwyn Davies was a student at the Bala-Bangor Theological College in Bangor and a prominent member of SCM. Spiritual impressions were made on him at the IVF campaign at Llanelli

J. Elwyn Davies

in 1945 and at the TSF Conference at Trinity College, Cambridge, where he listened to Dr Lloyd-Jones. In 1947 he came to faith in Christ at an SCM Easter retreat in Plas-y-nant, Betws Garmon. That same year he attended a World Youth Conference in Oslo and went from there to Germany. He was drawn for a time to do relief work in Germany and thought of abandoning his BD course. At that critical juncture Mr Owen Parry, a history specialist at Bangor, asked to see him and in the course of conversation remarked: 'If Wales does not recover the faith in *your* generation, many generations could pass by without it.'[9] The desire to go to Germany left him completely. This was the second turning point in his life, and it was also to be a turning point for the evangelical testimony in Wales.

Davies began to get opportunities to speak at churches in North Wales and was struck by the number of lonely Christians he came across. He engaged in evangelism in the Bala-Bangor College and news of conversions began to spread. A mission to the university was planned for Easter 1948. In preparation for this mission a 'retreat' was convened by Herbert Evans for Dolgellau in January 1948. The speaker was T. Arthur Pritchard. He referred to the 'hard' time at the start of the retreat but heart searching, which included Elwyn Davies, led to a change and the speaker recorded in his diary:

It is difficult to find words to express what happened at the end of the meeting. The Holy Spirit came down upon the company in a wonderful way. A new and strange experience, an unforgettable day.[10]

This gaining of spiritual momentum in the student world gave birth to a campaign in Bala at Easter 1948. The campaign leader was the Rev. I. D. E. Thomas, a former member of the IVF in Bangor. He was accompanied by Arthur Pritchard and Elwyn Davies. On the third night the Holy Spirit began to work powerfully in the hearts of many and the campaign bore lasting fruit in conversions, in revitalizing Christians and in a desire to strengthen the witness of the gospel. Dr Lloyd-Jones' interest went to the extent of inviting I. D. E. Thomas to London to hear at first hand details of the campaign. 'He felt at the time that something new was about to happen in the history of religion in Wales.'[11]

One way in which the work was strengthened was through the launch of a new magazine. At the end of the campaign four men — Arthur Pritchard, I. D. E. Thomas, Herbert Evans and J. Elwyn Davies — approached the owner of Seren Press in Bala. They told him of their vision to have an evangelical magazine in the Welsh language, emphasizing that they had neither movement, nor fund, nor patrons behind them — this was a venture of faith. An order was placed for printing 1500 copies. A small company of people met in Aberystwyth to discuss the magazine's content, decide on a title and choose its cover designer. The name finally agreed was *Y Cyclhgrawn Efengylaidd* (*The Evangelical Magazine*), which was to be issued bimonthly. The cover was a cross, the heart of the gospel, rising out of a Bible, the foundation of true faith. The first issue appeared in November-December 1948 and included a defining article by the Doctor on 'The Evangelical Faith', and seven pages of news were devoted to telling the exciting story of the years 1946-1948. J. Elwyn Davies was appointed secretary.[12]

A mission was planned for Bangor in January 1949, when they were able to secure Dr Lloyd-Jones as one of the preachers. It was a rare thing for the Doctor to lead a university mission but the impact on the college was enormous. Elwyn Davies was to be the spearhead in planning to hire a tent at the National Eisteddfod in Dolgellau in August 1949 for the distribution of the new magazine. An open-air meeting was held in the town square at night, followed by a service in one of the chapels at 11.30pm when Dr Lloyd-Jones gave a message. There developed a close tie between the work of the IVF and 'the people of the magazine'. These two were to be linked together through the person of J. Elwyn Davies, who became IVF's Travelling Secretary and later Secretary of the emerging Evangelical Movement of Wales.

For some years Dr Lloyd-Jones resisted the desire of others to launch a Welsh IVF Conference but during a leaders' conference at Swanwick in 1948, Welsh students sat down to plan such a conference the following year. They invited the Doctor to speak at what was to be the first of three conferences in successive years: 1949 — Borth; 1950 — Newcastle Emlyn; and 1951 — Borth. This was the first time that students, and especially theological students, came to grips with the expository power of the Doctor. The subject at the first conference was 'The biblical doctrine of man'; at the second he spoke on the Holy Spirit; and at the third the topic was 'The sovereignty of God'. Many men look back on that series of conference addresses as being the determining influence on their ministry. John B. E. Thomas of Sandfields said he gained more theology from the three series of addresses than from all his years in theological college.

The testimony of two other ministers shows something of the impact that was made at the time. Derek Swann, speaking of the third conference, said:

When Dr Lloyd-Jones spoke on the sovereignty of God, many of us came to the doctrines of grace for the first time, myself included. He left the doctrine of the sovereignty of God in *salvation* to his last talk, having in the previous two talks laid down all principles that he would apply in the final talk ... I remember it was early in the morning in conversation with Gwyn Walters that the truth of election dawned on me. I was so overcome with the wonder of it all that I had to fight back the tears. For many of us since, election has been an affair of the heart as well as the head. I've always been grateful to the Doctor for that. I believe we owe more than we realize for making it heart-warming stuff.[13]

Geraint Morgan commented:

On the last evening of the conference I came under a tremendous conviction of sin, and joining the queue to see Dr Martyn I reached him just after midnight. In that conference I yielded gladly my Arminian views and came to rejoice in the doctrines of sovereign grace.[14]

Dr Lloyd-Jones' own view of this has been recorded:

I felt God's hand was on these young men. I liked their approach and, having come to see the conference was justified, it was important that it had a Welsh character about it. It also gave the opportunity to stay the influence of higher criticism and evolutionism... Several of the younger men now saw the campaigns and the conference as servants of the church. Under God they were used to produce evangelical ministers, and to a lesser extent, evangelical churches. The particularly happy thing about the Welsh IVF circles was that it re-oriented back to the church and men found their fellowship there.[15]

Welsh Annual Conference, Denbigh, 1955

In second row, seated, Bethan Lloyd-Jones, Dr Martyn Lloyd-Jones, I. D. E. Thomas, J. Elwyn Davies, T. Arthur Pritchard, Emyr Roberts, Herbert Evans

Following the launch of the Welsh-language bimonthly magazine in 1948, many of its readers were meeting in 'evangelical fellowships'. The need was felt for an annual gathering and the first Welsh-language conference was held in Bala, 11-14 August 1952. The non-Welsh speakers and English felt they needed a conference as well and this was arranged in 1957 for Sandfields, Aberavon, where John Thomas ministered. The main speaker was Dr Lloyd-Jones, whose addresses on Ephesians 3:14-19 were 'emphatically God-centred'. After the first conference the venue shifted to Aberystwyth where it has remained. Attendance grew steadily over the years requiring the use of larger premises, until eventually it was the university campus with its increased residential accommodation and its Great Hall that met the demands of the occasion. Geraint Fielder speaks of Aberystwyth in the 1960s as having 'an unparalleled liveliness of evangelical witness in town and College'. One of the contributors to this was 'the new and arresting ministry of Geoffrey Thomas at Alfred Place Baptist Church'. Geoff had been converted while at Cardiff University and went on to study at Westminster Theological Seminary in the USA. The life and teaching of Professor John Murray left an indelible impression on his life and future ministry. His contributions to the work of the Evangelical Movement of Wales, the Banner of Truth Trust, the Puritan Conference, the Carey Conference and conferences on both sides of the Atlantic have assisted greatly in the recovery of the Reformed vision.

Another sequel to the start of the English conferences should be mentioned here as a indication of the growing link between Christians in England and Wales. Elizabeth Braund, the daughter of an English judge, had become interested in Christianity through researching for the preparation of a BBC programme on Mildred Cable, the missionary to China. She began reading the New Testament and eventually came to faith in Christ under the ministry of Dr Lloyd-Jones. While attending the 1957 conference in Aberavon she suggested the launch in England of a magazine similar to the Welsh one. Discussions took place with J. Elwyn Davies and Dr Lloyd-Jones and they even considered such a magazine for Scotland and Ireland. A meeting of leaders was held in Bala in April 1958. It is referred to in a letter from the Doctor to Elwyn Davies dated 5 May 1958.

Due to his heavy commitments the Doctor withdrew from the committee, while remaining supportive of the venture. Elizabeth Braund and Elwyn Davies joined with Dr Jim Packer to further the plan, and they became joint editors. The first issue of *The Evangelical Magazine* appeared in September 1959 and it was to be issued bimonthly. It was there that Dr Packer's series on 'Knowing God', later to become a spiritual classic, first appeared. A feature of the magazine was that it contained a supplement listing the 'Area Meetings for Bible Ministry' in England and Ireland. The one in my possession for June 1969 lists thirty-seven such meetings in England, with only one in Northern Ireland.

The Westminster Fellowship: 'the Pastor's Pastor'

Dr Lloyd-Jones possessed a dislike of organization. He is reputed to have said that the Ministers' Fellowship at Sandfields was the only new thing which he had ever begun. What he did for the furtherance of the gospel was generally due to the organization of others into which he entered. This appears to be what happened with the Westminster Fellowship, which began in 1941 as a quarterly Tuesday morning meeting intended for pastors and men in positions of Christian leadership. The inspiration came from the indefatigable Dr Douglas Johnson and in the light of ministerial contacts he made through the Inter-Varsity Fellowship. Attendance was only by invitation and the numbers were low.

The gathering was augmented in early 1942. The Rev. Alan Stibbs was leading a small IVF study group in central London, when they reached a point of difficulty with respect to the doctrine of original sin. A paper which had been prepared by Dr Philip E. Hughes (1915-90) on the subject was sent by the Rev. Stibbs to Dr Lloyd-Jones for his comment. This was the first contact that was to lead to a lasting friendship between Hughes and Lloyd-Jones. In a letter dated 3 February 1942, Dr Lloyd-Jones expressed the view that Hughes was the type of scholar and writer he had been looking for and then refers to the fraternal: 'A number of us, including Mr Stibbs, have started a new fellowship of evangelical ministers and clergy. I have suggested that all of you who meet with Mr Stibbs be invited.'[16] Alan Stibbs acted as secretary.

Another contact made by the Doctor about this time was with the Rev. Ernest F. Kevan, pastor of Zion Baptist Church in New Cross, London, which belonged to the Metropolitan Association of Strict Baptist Churches. They discovered their mutual love for the Puritan authors. Kevan also became a member of the Westminster Fellowship and was added to the committee of the Evangelical Library in June 1943. A further project in which the Doctor was involved was the London Bible College. Plans were in hand by 1942 and it was hoped that Dr Lloyd-Jones would become the Principal, but he declined. He had difficulty thinking of a candidate holding his own theology but in the end proposed Ernest Kevan. This was accepted and Kevan began working part time in January 1944. By the time the college was settled at 19 Marylebone Road in 1946, Kevan was the Principal, a position he held until his death in 1965. He was also fully involved in the formative years of the Puritan Conference.

To return to the Westminster Fellowship, by 1955 the numbers were such that they had to move from the parlour to the much larger Institute Hall in Westminster Chapel. By then there was an annual day's outing each June. Towards the end of the decade the venue for the outing became the old manor house of 'Guessens' at Welwyn, with its gardens and an evangelical church nearby for the meetings. In the early 1960s the meetings moved to the first Monday of the month, and consisted of a morning and afternoon session. Differences over attitudes to the ecumenical movement and membership of mixed denominations caused division in the fellowship and the matter was ultimately resolved by the fellowship being re-constituted in early 1967. The Doctor continued to lead the meetings until June 1980.

We have an insight into the working of the fellowship from the Rev. Dr Hywel Jones in 'The Pastor's Pastor' which he contributed to the volume *Martyn Lloyd-Jones: Chosen By God.* He described it as a 'finishing school' for ministers and claimed that 'the Doctor made those who had the irreplaceable privilege of being members of the Westminster Fellowship *ready for life'*. The pattern usually followed in the meeting was quite open. Any member could raise a question for discussion and it was the practice for a theological subject to be taken up in the morning and a pastoral one in the afternoon.

Such an arrangement had many benefits. First the need for ministers to be continuing students of theology was underlined, yet the need to be truly pastoral was not minimized... The chief benefit of such a pattern to the meeting lay in having the Doctor's responses to the matters raised. These would be given at the beginning, in the course of and at the end of the discussion.

In conclusion Dr Hywel Jones said, 'Many of us found in that meeting what we had not gained in university or theological college.'[17]

It was not only in the Westminster Fellowship that ministers benefited from the Doctor's counsel. In his travels throughout the UK and on the telephone he would be helping men with personal and pastoral problems. Dr Douglas Johnson, who was the inspiration behind the formation of the fellowship, wrote, on hearing of the Doctor's retirement from the chapel, a very warm letter of tribute to him. The concluding paragraph reads:

Whatever eternity may reveal of the effect of your actual ministry (and public addresses all over the country, church anniversaries, 'big meetings' and inductions etc.), I myself would say that one of the most valuable services to the country as a whole will prove to be the encouraging and advising, in a number of forms, of young ministers. I do not mean so much the Westminster Fellowship meetings but *personal* reassurances, personal advice, and advice on preaching to the young newly ordained ministers in little difficult churches without much real fellowship. *This* attention to the candlesticks twinkling in the inhospitable country and dreary townships has been a truly important and, in influence, worthwhile action.[18]

I have a hope that God has a purpose for these precious writings beyond what we yet realize. Will the dawn of a fresh day of God's power, such as George Whitefield knew, bring with it a far greater interest in the rich heritage of spiritual works which are here preserved and shall we have yet more abundant reason to bless God that he brought this work into existence? Pray that it may be so and that the Holy Spirit will descend upon us and bring about such a blessing.

GEOFFREY WILLIAMS (1961)

It is our hope that this re-awakened interest in works that represent a warmer, a more reverential, and a more spiritually intelligent understanding of the Gospel, may herald a coming visitation of grace amongst the people of God, now so urgently needed. It is not infrequently one of the first evidences of a movement of God upon the soul that a man begins to turn to books that correspond to his new-born sense of need.

E. J. POOLE-CONNOR (1959)

Geoffrey Williams

5.

Geoffrey Williams: 'the storehouse'

The story of how Geoffrey Williams (1886-1975) was inspired to collect Christian books for loan that eventually lead to the establishment of the Evangelical Library is perhaps one of the most romantic episodes in the whole account of the Reformed recovery. As Mr Williams himself recalled the providences that occurred to establish the work of the library, including a life-changing meeting with Dr Lloyd-Jones, he would refer to each step as 'on a certain day'.

Encouraged to read good books

'On a certain day' in 1903 Geoffrey Williams, at the request of a schoolgirl, went to a service at Galeed Chapel, Brighton, a Strict Baptist congregation of 'Gospel Standard' persuasion. The preacher was Pastor J. K. Popham. He recounted the incident on more than one occasion:

> The day was bleak and the sky lowering as 'gamp' [umbrella] in hand I wended my way to Galeed Chapel, Brighton. It was the first time in my life that I had approached a place of worship where the truth was proclaimed and I

had no taste for the prospect. Hilda, a girl friend of my own age, had urged me to go for she had prayed for my salvation. Pride caused me to suppose I could 'walk out' if the preacher displeased me and in this frame I reached the door a flagrant sinner, blind to my condition.[1]

On another occasion he recalled the means used in his conversion at that time:

God was pleased to arrest my soul and convict me of sin through a hymn in that little Strict Baptist Chapel in Brighton called Galeed to which I was led to go at the age of sixteen. The hymn was by Samuel Medley:

> A beggar poor, at mercy's door,
> Lies such a wretch as I;
> Thou know'st my need is great indeed
> Lord, hear me when I cry.[2]

After his conversion he says he began to 'long for grace and wisdom to render unto my dear Saviour some measure of service in the salvation of souls'. It was through Mr Popham's ministry that Williams was first directed to read good books. These included Bunyan's *Pilgrim's Progress*, Rutherford's *Letters* and David Brainerd's *Journal*, as well as some Puritan authors. The love for the doctrines he discovered in these authors led Mr Williams to collect their works. 'Having neither gift nor "call" for preaching, I felt constrained to collect and loan books reflecting the love of Christ.' Seeing the help which the books proved to be to Christian friends, he felt an irresistible urge to provide 'a widespread loan library fitted to enable people everywhere to borrow books true to Scripture, calculated to bring sinners to the foot of the Cross and to establish Christians in our most holy faith'.

Old second-hand books of spiritual worth were at that time comparatively plentiful, as well as little valued. Geoffrey Williams became like Joseph in the land of Egypt, laying up stores for the famine years which lay ahead. He was later to recall those early days:

> When I began collecting books for this undertaking, the Puritan authors were one of my two chief quests, the other was for books on true revivals of religion and in particular the Great Awakening in the eighteenth century, under George Whitefield, Daniel Rowland, Howell Harris and other like-minded men. I had a burden for revival and I shall never forget the cries that went up to God as I walked along the railway bank pathway near the spot where the idea of this now world-wide Library first came to me.[3]

Geoffrey Williams had already recognized the anomaly of a Protestant nation which possessed a variety of specialist information libraries but lacked a national repository of the best in Protestant evangelical literature. He had also realized that many excellent evangelical works were fast disappearing from the public domain, and so he set himself the task of reclaiming as many of them as possible as a heritage for future generations. With the seed thus sown in his mind, Geoffrey Williams systematically scoured the length and breadth of the nation in pursuit of a wide range of important books for the collection.

The books he collected were accommodated first in his own home, known as 'The Brandries' in Beddington, twelve miles from London. It is interesting to note that Mr S. M. Houghton was in attendance at the home in 1924 as 'certain ministers preached in his house at week-evening services', but strangely he records, 'I saw nothing of Mr Williams' famous library.'[4] The library expanded to a garage and then to a few 'do it yourself' sheds. Later the library was moved to a brick building in Wordsworth

Road in Beddington. It was there that the 'Beddington Free Grace Library', as it was then called, was born and had its first public meeting in 1933. A small group of men of the Strict and Particular Baptist persuasion supported the work of the library. Once a year there was an afternoon for special services in the local chapel and on those occasions the favourite preacher was Frederick Kirby, the pastor at Staplehurst in Kent. It was on a sheet announcing the services at the chapel on 3 March 1931 that the first printed news of 'The Beddington Free Grace Library' appeared: 'Owing to the generosity of several friends it is believed to be the most comprehensive lending library of Free Grace books in existence.'[5]

A committee was formed and Mr Kirby was appointed the library's first president. He made his own contribution by donating thirty parcels of old and rare books to the new venture. Pastor Fred Windridge (1867-1961), another member of the committee, concluded his address at the opening meeting in 1933 by 'expressing the hope that it may please God to make Beddington Library a real blessing in all parts of the English-

Beddington Free Grace Library

speaking world. These men combined love for the old Calvinistic truths with a real measure of catholicity.

In a letter sent just before his death, Mr Kirby wrote as follows to Mr Williams:

> The Library will be a blessing to the Church of Christ, not only now but after our heads are laid beneath the clods of the valley. Had God not prospered this work in your hands there never could have been such a collection of Puritan and Free Grace works gathered together under one roof. I have felt this matter laid upon my heart in prayer before God.

One can see how the death of Mr Kirby in 1934 was a special loss to the library, and indeed Mr Williams spoke of it as closing the first chapter in its history. Speaking in later days about the year 1937 he refers to it as 'a time when I was travelling a dark and thorny pathway' and how 'a simple sentence found a mark never to be erased from my heart'. It was from the Rev. G. A. Bliss (vicar of Loddiswell, South Devon) and the words were 'The Library is ordained of God'.

His testimony continued:

> If there is one soul to whom the Library has proved a mighty blessing it is surely me … it is a literal and spiritual mine of sound and profound theology and the bells have never ceased ringing in my soul since your precious books came to me.[6]

Meeting Dr Martyn Lloyd-Jones

It was to be ten years before the next chapter in the history of the library would begin but in the interval came the vital link with

Dr Martyn Lloyd-Jones. The Beddington location was too far away in the country for Londoners to use it and during the mid-1930s there was no increase in the readership. 'On a certain day' in 1938 Mr Williams was walking down Great Portland Street in London, when he went into a chemist's shop to make a small purchase. The owner, Mr John Philips, was a Welshman and a member of the Charing Cross Calvinistic Methodist Chapel. Mr Williams recalls:

> I was attracted by his Welsh accent and getting into conversation with him I opened my heart to him in regard to the difficulty I faced. He at once exclaimed, 'Why you must meet Dr Martyn Lloyd-Jones. His interest will be aroused and he will suggest a way out. I will tell him about your project.'[7]

That day was a major turning point in the life of Mr Williams and the library. Mr Philips fulfilled his promise and not long after that Dr Lloyd-Jones, accompanied by the Rev. Eliseus Howells, made a visit to the library in Beddington. Writing to Mr Williams on 4 September 1939 he said,

> Having arrived and spent two and a half hours inspecting the contents, I felt that I was in the precise position of the Queen of Sheba on the occasion of her visit to Solomon. The collection is remarkable and indeed unique. As far as I am aware, there is, and can be, no such collection of books anywhere.

He went on:

> I have but one criticism to offer, and that is with regard to the location of the Library. It should be somewhere in the heart of London within easy reach and access.[8]

It was to be another six years before the library was established in London. With the outbreak of the Second World War in 1939 difficulties increased. Possibilities considered for the future of the library included selling off the most valuable parts to dealers, passing on the library to the newly formed London Bible College, or even shipping it to America. But as Mr Williams kept pressing for a decision on a move, the Doctor enlisted the help of Dr Douglas Johnson, the General Secretary of the IVF. He visited the library and he too was impressed by the collection of books. By October 1942 Dr Johnson had arranged a small committee. Mr Williams and another three men met at the Kingsley Hotel in London on 15 December. The agenda read: 'Consideration of value of Library to Christendom (and especially to the Evangelical School of thought) and what steps can be taken to: a) Secure it, free of all claims, for the Church of God; (b) Centralize it; (c) Finance the running of it as an active organization.'[9]

The library moves to London

The only minister present on that occasion, and the only one on the small committee possessed of some influence, was the stalwart 'defender of the faith', Rev. E. J. Poole-Connor. He was destined to play a major part in the future development of the library. Dr Lloyd-Jones was hesitant to get involved because of the uncertainty of his own position at Westminster Chapel. However by June 1943 the Doctor had agreed to become President of the library and so committed himself to what was to prove for him a life work. He was in the chair for two meetings in the vestry of Westminster Chapel, when the committee was augmented by the Rev. Eliseus Howells and the Rev. Ernest F. Kevan. A trust deed was settled and the name 'The Evangelical Library' unanimously agreed. The library was to be housed at premises in 55 Gloucester Road, South Kensington, London, for an annual rent of £70.

After various obstacles had been overcome, the Beddington Library, consisting of 25,000 books and weighing fifteen tons, was transported to London. It was the veteran Rev. E. J. Poole-Connor, now in his early seventies, along with a friend, who put up most of the shelving in the building. The inaugural meeting was on 15 January 1945, when the Doctor remarked: 'It is the founder's desire, in which we fully concur, that this Library should become not a museum but a living force.' So Reformed books of a type which before the war had been scarcely saleable were now within easy access in London. The membership subscription was 6s 6d, and by VE Day, 250 people had joined the library.

The year 1945 was indeed a new beginning for the library. The first *Evangelical Library Bulletin* appeared. It summarized the aims of the library in three words: 'Preservation, Information, Circulation'. These words became a permanent subtitle in library promotion literature. In what may have been the first article to appear by a member of the committee, Dr Ernest Kevan said:

It provided new facilities for the reading of evangelical literature; but more than that it aimed to bring the very existence of this vast field of literature to the notice of those to whom it was always unknown, and supremely it was to promote the doctrines which that distinctive literature contains.[10]

The occupation of the premises in Gloucester Road did not last more than two years. 'On a certain day', Prebendary Colin Kerr telephoned Mr Williams to say that he had a big building available near Baker Street Station, where the library could expand. The building belonged to St Paul's Church, Portman Square, where the Rev. Kerr was the vicar, and was used formerly as a school and a dispensary. In October 1946 the library moved to the premises at 78 Chiltern Street, off Marylebone Road, parallel to Baker Street and not far from the well-known Madame Tussaud's. It was a Victorian building with ground and two upper floors joined by a stone staircase. The library was housed on the top floor. Again the Rev. E. J. Poole-Connor got to work in preparing the shelving for the ever-increasing number of books.

Current premises of Evangelical Library taken in 1986

By 1948, as we see from a leaflet advertising the library, a pattern was set which was to be followed for the subsequent years. The 'annual business meeting' was to be held in the library on Tuesday 30 November at 5.30pm with 'Preview of the Library during the afternoon'. This was to be followed by a 'Public Meeting at the Welsh Chapel, 82 Chiltern Street, Baker Street Station at 6.30pm when the Inauguration of the Friends of the Evangelical Library will be followed by a lecture by the Rev. Dr D. Martyn Lloyd-Jones on Isaac Watts and Hymnody in Worship. Chairman: Rev. E. J. Poole-Connor'. No record of this lecture appears to have survived.[11] The annual business meeting continued to be held in the library in late November or early December, but the time of the annual lecture in the Welsh Chapel was changed to early summer.

Library expansion

By 1948 the library had acquired most of the first floor, which was accessed by a back stair from the library floor. This is where the branch activity was centred. Following the vision given to the early founders for worldwide distribution, branch libraries were formed all over the globe. It is believed that the first one was founded in Switzerland in 1946. By 1954 there were 'no less than eighty' branches. Some were combined with other evangelical agencies or attached to colleges, while others were the result of missionary endeavour, as in the case of 'our missionary in the Congo, Madeleine Bremond from Switzerland'.

Looking after the branch work was Monsieur Gabriel Godet, a nephew of the great Swiss commentator, who began helping in the work in 1953. He was assisted by Mr H. Bucknell and Mr W. Gurden. The latter was packing books for the branches while he was still in his nineties. At the annual meeting in 1960 Mr Williams could report that a total of 84,077 books had been sent to overseas branches.

There is an interesting assessment of the library work by E. J. Poole-Connor in the *Evangelical Library Bulletin* in autumn 1959:

Those who have had the privilege of being associated with the Evangelical Library from its early days have no possible doubt that it is — to use an old-fashioned phrase — a work of God. They believe this to have been demonstrated in a variety of ways. There is for instance the phenomenal growth of the number of volumes to be found on its shelves. When the writer of these lines first became acquainted with it, these did not exceed 24,000; today they amount in round figures to 100,000; and still they increase.

Mr Poole-Connor went on to speak about creating the spiritual desire for books:

> There is, however, an aspect of the Library's services to the cause of Evangelicalism to which we here desire to call special attention. It is that of *creating a taste* for the high order of spiritual literature which it is the responsibility of this unique institution to supply ... It began to be clear that it was manifestly part of the Library's work not merely to supply access to evangelical literature, but to create and educate the mental and spiritual desire for it... Of religious books in general there is no lack... The outstanding need of the day is wise guidance in the choice of reading matter.[12]

When the present writer arrived in London in June 1960 to work in the editorial department of the Banner of Truth Trust, he had to find a 'working space' in the reference room of the Evangelical Library, due to limitations on the office space downstairs. It was there I came to appreciate the vast wealth of Puritan literature. The rare volumes were housed in the reference room and in the glass-fronted cases that were high above the lending shelves accessible to the public. The rarest volumes were in what was known as 'the Robinson Collection'. Some of the books I was preparing for reprinting by the trust had been taken off the library shelves. The books that had been carefully collected and housed by Geoffrey Williams over many years were now taking on a new life.

It was from that vantage point that I came to appreciate the contribution that the staff of the library were making. In the little office at the entrance sat Mr Geoffrey Williams, with his faithful and hard-working secretary, Miss Marjorie Denby. It was part of Miss Denby's job to check on visitors as they appeared at the

Reference Room with Geoffrey Williams

window of the office. If it was a familiar face her nod indicated 'you may pass through the gate'; if it was someone unknown to her, questions were asked and the name had to be entered in the visitor's book. If it was someone seeking some information about an author or a book, he or she might well be passed on to Mr M. J. Micklewright, a beloved deacon at Westminster Chapel, whose operational desk was in the first bay of the library. Mr Micklewright was a 'walking encyclopedia' on the Puritan authors but was known on occasions to be involved in some heated theological debate with an individual — the words being carried across the partition-less library.

The one name that seemed to pass most frequently from everyone's lips in the library was that of 'the Doctor'. He was the President and there would be phone calls from him asking the staff to trace this volume or that. When the books requested were found they were usually carried by Miss Denby in a net bag on the Friday evening (Westminster Chapel Bible Study night) and duly delivered to the Doctor's vestry. The appearances of the Doctor in the library itself were mainly confined to the days when there were meetings of the committee. My closest contact with him in the early days came on those occasions. There was always an air of preparation and anticipation as the library staff awaited the arrival of the Doctor, usually shortly after 5.00pm. He would invariably appear in some haste with overcoat on and hat firmly in his hand.

It was while engaged in my work there that I first caught sight of some of the other distinguished members of the committee — E. J. Poole-Connor, Ernest F. Kevan, Gordon Savage (Bishop of Buckingham), Alan M. Stibbs, and J. C. Doggett. Six years after my first introduction to the Evangelical Library I was invited to become a member of the committee. It was a privilege to serve the library in that capacity from 1966 until, after my moving to Edinburgh in 1972, it was no longer easy to attend meetings.

As redwoods attract the eye because they overtop other trees, so the mature holiness and seasoned fortitude of the great Puritans shine before us as a kind of beacon light, overtopping the stature of the majority of Christians in most eras, and certainly so in this age of crushing urban collectivism.

JAMES I. PACKER

Dr James I. Packer

6.

James I. Packer: 'among God's giants'

It is probably true to say that of the younger men who gathered around Dr Lloyd-Jones in the early days of the recovery of the Reformed vision the most significant at the time was James I. Packer.

In Packer's background and education there are interesting parallels with the eighteenth-century evangelist George Whitefield. Like the great revivalist he was born in Gloucester. His grandfather, who was a gentleman farmer from Oxfordshire, became the landlord of a tavern in Gloucestershire. His father, James Percy Packer, was a clerk with the Great Western Railway Company, and his mother, Dorothy Mary Packer, was a schoolteacher. The couple had two children: a daughter, Margaret, born in 1929; and a son, James Innel Packer, who was born on 22 July 1926. The place of his birth meant that James carried with him into adult life a distinctive 'West Country burr' and a great affection for steam trains.

Early life

James began to attend the National School in Gloucester in 1933. He was a shy and awkward boy who found it difficult to relate to other children. At the school he was being bullied, and one day another boy pushed him out of the school grounds on to a busy road. A passing bread van could not avoid hitting him. He was thrown to the ground and sustained a major head injury. It was a near fatal accident which caused damage to the frontal lobe of his brain. After skilful surgery he recovered, but the injury left him with a small hole in the right side of his forehead which would remain clearly visible for the rest of his life. He was away from school for six months and was unable to join in with normal schoolboy activities.

Being naturally reserved, James found solace in solitary things. He became 'something of a bookworm'. Accompanying his father to the railway office on Saturdays he was allowed to use a typewriter. When it came near to the time of his eleventh birthday he was dropping hints that he would like a bicycle. However, with the head injury his parents knew this was not for him. When the day came, and the present was awaiting him in the dining room, it turned out to be an Oliver typewriter.

It was not more than a minute before he had put paper into the machine and had started to type. It proved to be his best present and the most treasured possession of his boyhood.[1]

In 1937 he moved on to the Crypt School, where George Whitefield had been a pupil, and where one of the houses was named after the distinguished alumnus. Like Whitefield he was brought up in the Anglican Church. St Catherine's Church, where his parents attended, had been influenced by the Anglo-Catholic 'revival' of the nineteenth century. The teaching James received from the curate before his confirmation reflected the typical form of Tractarianism, which consisted in the need for personal devotion, preparation for Holy Communion and the importance of personal morality. Conversion did not come into it.

James was stirred to an interest in Christianity in a strange way. He began to play chess at school with Brian Bone, the son of a local Unitarian minister, who attempted to convert Packer to Unitarianism. The debates raised in Packer's mind the whole question of the truth of Christianity. In his sixth-form class he was introduced to the recently published *Screwtape Letters* by C. S. Lewis. This gave him a taste for the writings of Lewis and reinforced his growing interest in the truth of Christianity. Another schoolboy friend also had an influence on him. Eric Taylor went to the University of Bristol where he was converted through the ministry of the Christian Union. He wrote to his old school friend Jim and tried to explain what had happened. Packer was not convinced but accepted Taylor's suggestion that he get in touch with the Christian Union at Oxford University when he arrived there.

Student at Oxford

In 1943 Packer had sat an examination for a scholarship in classics to go to Corpus Christi College, Oxford, and was successful, although he was advised to remain in school for another year. Eventually, in October 1944, Packer left his parents' home to begin life at one of the world's most famous universities, a journey undertaken by Whitefield over 200 years before. 'By the time I went up to Oxford I wanted reality', said Packer.[2] Before he could make contact with the Christian Union, Ralph Hume of the Oxford Inter-Collegiate Christian Union (OICCU) sought him out and invited him to the 'fresher's squash'. It was the second Sunday of term before he attended the evangelistic service. That evening it was held in St Aldate's Church in the city, where the sermon was preached by the Rev. Earl Langston, an elderly Church of England minister from Weymouth in Dorset. The first half of the sermon left Packer unmoved. It was in the second half, when Langston told of his own conversion, that Packer realized that he was not a Christian. In response to the call of the need to come to Christ, James I. Packer made his personal commitment. The place where it happened was about 100 feet from where fellow citizen, George Whitefield, had done so in 1735.

Packer became an active member of OICCU, attending the Bible study and the daily prayer meetings. On Sundays he worshipped at St Aldate's, one of two evangelical Church of England congregations in the centre of Oxford. Returning home to Gloucester for the holiday at the end of the first term he was determined not to waste time. Although he had attended the same school as Whitefield and been converted in the same city, he knew virtually nothing of the great evangelist. He recalls the time:

> When I became a Christian in 1944, Whitefield's role in the evangelical life of his day was unknown to those who nurtured me. But I knew his name, for I attended his old school, the Crypt School, Gloucester, and had seen him represented in a school pageant (not very accurately, as I later learned) hammering sabbath-breakers. Three months after my conversion, lying in bed with bronchitis, I read both volumes of Luke Tyerman's 1876 biography, and the career of the great Gloucestrian made a tremendous impression on me, securing him pride of place in my private heroes gallery. I subsequently found that Whitefield had made a similar impact on C. H. Spurgeon, the nineteenth century's greatest pastoral evangelist, and on Martyn Lloyd-Jones, Spurgeon's nearest twentieth-century counterpart.[3]

The encounter with Whitefield was a milestone in his spiritual journey. He would refer later to Whitefield as 'the startling Puritan'. It was not long before Packer would discover for himself the writings of the seventeenth-century Puritans.

Discovering John Owen

Evangelicalism in England in the 1940s was dominated by what was known as the 'Keswick teaching on sanctification'. This took its rise from the 'Convention for the Deepening of the Spiritual Life' which had begun in the town of Keswick in the Lake District, in 1875. By the 1940s the Keswick teaching had come to be seen as a distinctive article of evangelical belief. The teaching offered deliverance from the power of sin and a closer relationship to Christ. The key to this victorious living was the Christian's full surrender to Christ. The teaching was prevalent in the OICCU circles in Oxford. During 1945 Packer found himself deeply troubled by this view. He discovered that his attempts at full surrender and total consecration seemed to leave him where he was. The only remedy his teachers could offer was 'to let go and let God'.

It was while feeling the tension between this brand of teaching and his own Christian experience that Packer discovered the seventeenth-century English Puritans. This came about through having to handle books which were the gift of a minister's library to OICCU. It belonged to a clergyman of the Church of England, C. Owen Pickard-Cambridge, who had been at one time vice-principal of the Bible Churchman's College in Bristol (later Tyndale Hall). He had acquired a large collection of books, many being classics of the sixteenth and seventeenth centuries. Going blind and in his eighties he wished to dispose of his library, but rather than break up the collection he gave it in its entirety to OICCU in 1944.

The books were stored in the basement of North Gate Hall, which was used for the OICCU daily prayer meetings. The Rev.

John Reynolds was the Senior Librarian of OICCU at the time. He recalled that James Packer was something of a bookworm, so the collection was entrusted to him. He became junior librarian for OICCU in 1945. As Packer sorted through the dusty piles of books he came across an uncut set of the writings of the Puritan John Owen, which had been published in twenty-four volumes by W. H. Goold during the years 1850-55. As he came to volume six he was struck particularly by the titles of two treatises, *On Indwelling Sin in Believers* and *On the Mortification of Sin in Believers.* He began to cut the pages and to read what he found there.

OICCU members gathered at St Ebbe's Rectory, 1948

James Packer is in the third row, seventh from right; and Elizabeth Lloyd-Jones (now Lady Catherwood) is immediately in front of Packer

He was attracted by the realism of Owen's analysis, both of the problems arising from indwelling sin and the means of dealing with it. Packer had found a man who spoke to his condition and offered a realistic solution. He felt at this time 'a very isolated person'. Later on, he concluded that the followers of the Keswick teaching were either 'very insensitive' or 'very good at kidding themselves' that they could obey all God's laws. Packer then discovered Bishop J. C. Ryle's classic book on *Holiness* and found that Ryle based much of his teaching on the Puritans.[4]

This discovery in a basement of the North Gate Hall marked a turning point in Packer's Christian life and indeed had implications for others who shared that interest. One was O. Raymond Johnston, studying Modern Languages at Queen's College, and another was Elizabeth Lloyd-Jones, elder daughter of Dr Martyn Lloyd-Jones. They were the core of a group that began meeting on Wednesday evenings in the Michaelmas term of 1946. Packer later wrote how 'he belonged to a group which used to eat cheap food in a British Restaurant and talked about revival; also about Calvin, Owen, the Welsh evangelical heritage and the Puritans.'[5]

The truths that Packer discovered could not be found in any local Christian bookshop. Donald Wiseman recalls a conversation with Packer at this time in which he expresses his view that there was not enough good evangelical literature available. The enthusiasm for the Puritan inheritance began to surface and the new note was first struck by Raymond Johnston. The IVF magazine for the summer term 1948 carried an article by him entitled 'John Owen: a Puritan Vice-Chancellor'. But although that kind of theology was not available in Christian bookshops at the time it was being preached by Dr Martyn Lloyd-Jones at Westminster Chapel in London. As we have seen in the previous chapter, it was in the second half of the 1940s that the Doctor's influence among students and graduates reached its height. He was preaching for the various Christian Unions in the universities, speaking at conferences of the Theological Students' Fellowship and addressing graduates. Packer recalls hearing the Doctor at the TSF Conference at St Hugh's College in December 1946 on the theme of the authority of the Bible: 'He struck me as grim and austere, but vastly impressive, with his magisterial mind and intense seriousness.'[6]

The Puritan Conference

It was not long before Packer and Johnston were to have the opportunity to hear the Doctor preach on a regular basis, when both men exchanged Oxford for London. Packer had the assignment for the academic year 1948-49 as tutor in New Testament Greek in Oak Hill College, London, and attended Westminster Chapel on Sunday evenings. The preaching of the Doctor, he said, was like hearing 'a full orchestra after listening to a piano solo'.

In a letter to Iain Murray in 1981 he recalls:

> I was able to hear Dr Lloyd-Jones preach his way through Matthew 11. I had never heard such preaching and was electrified. I can remember at least the thrust of most of the messages still... All that I know about preaching I can honestly say — indeed I have often said — I learned from the Doctor by example that winter.[7]

He could say that this ministry taught him the greatness of God and the greatness of the soul.

Raymond Johnston, who was doing further study in London, was able to attend all the meetings at Westminster Chapel, including the discussion meeting on Friday evenings. Packer and Johnston, both members of the IVF's 'Tyndale Fellowship for Biblical Research', and full of their new-found interest in the

Puritans, had the idea of a conference with a particular focus on Puritan thought and life. It was clear that Dr Lloyd-Jones was ideally placed to promote such a venture, if his support could be secured. Dr Packer recalls his own first meeting with the Doctor along with Raymond Johnston in the vestry at Westminster Chapel:

> I was struck at the time by the air of suppressed excitement with which he welcomed the idea, as well as his extreme forthcomingness: not only would he host us at Westminster Chapel, but he would be permanent chairman.

Years later the Doctor told Packer that the interest the two young men had shown in publicizing Puritan standards of faith and devotion was 'one of the series of signs that God was starting to revive His work in Britain and therefore he had given all the backing he could'.[8]

A notice about the conference first appeared in the June issue of *The Christian Graduate* as follows:

> December 19-20, Tyndale Fellowship Conference at Westminster Chapel, 'The Distinctive Theological Contribution of the English Puritans'. Speakers include Rev. Dr Martyn Lloyd-Jones.

In the September issue of the same magazine James Packer wrote on 'The Doctrinal Puritans and their Work'. He contrasted the Puritans' thorough treatment of Christian experience with 'an endemic subjectivity in much modern teaching on the Christian life'. At the end of the article was a postscript drawing attention to a conference to be held at Westminster Chapel, 19-20 December 1950, under the general title 'The Distinctive Theological Contribution of the English Puritans'.[9]

There were not many more than twenty at the first conference. The young men, mostly graduates, took part with the enthusiasm of those possessed with a great discovery. Writing of those early days James Packer has said:

> I simply wanted to share what my own reading had taught me, and I was quite happy with the 20 or so folk who came on that first occasion. The Doctor, however, with whom as conference organiser I was now conversing for the first time, made no secret of his belief that what we were doing was of great potential importance for the Church: which struck me, for I never really thought of it that way.[10]

Although the regular pattern for the conference was to be six sessions over two days it appears that there were seven addresses given at the first one. Both David Fountain and Alister McGrath speak of Dr Packer giving three addresses. It appears that one of them was the closing address which may have been a summing up. His subject in the opening address was 'Historical and theological introduction'. Doctor Lloyd-Jones spoke on 'Puritan preaching'. David Fountain recalls the occasion:

> It dealt with Thomas Goodwin's exposition of Isaiah 50:10-11, on the subject 'A Child of Light Walking in Darkness and a Child of Darkness Walking in the Light'. It had a stunning effect upon me which lasted for some time. I had not appreciated the biblical doctrine of assurance and the Puritan view was shattering.

The other subjects and speakers were: 'The Puritan Use of the Old Testament' by O. Raymond Johnston; 'The Christian Life' by J. B. L. Gee; and 'Pastoral Theology' by C. L. L. Binder.[11]

It was almost inevitable that the conference should be nicknamed 'The Puritan Conference'. Packer became the organizer, but he recruited a young student, David Fountain, who went up to Oxford in the autumn of 1951, to be the secretary. David attended the first conference at the invitation of his pastor, Dr Lloyd-Jones. It appears that there were no reports of the early conferences and no attempt to reproduce the addresses. What is available by way of information came from David Fountain, and was published in recent years in a booklet entitled *Puritan Principles.*

> I did not make any notes of the first conference but extensive ones of 1951, 1952 and 1953, which I still have. It was not until 1954 that the papers were reproduced, these notes are the only source of information available and I am glad to have been asked to reproduce them.[12]

We learn from David Fountain's recollections that 'numbers grew from about thirty to double that in three years, then they reached a peak of 400 registrations in 1959'. From 1954 to 1957 the papers presented were reproduced in duplicated form and some men treasure these original editions. In 1958, for the first time, the papers given at the conference were printed under the title *A Goodly Heritage.* In the foreword Dr Packer explains that 'This booklet contains shortened versions of the six papers read at the 1958 Conference of the Puritan and Reformed Studies Group of the Tyndale Fellowship for Biblical Research'. He goes on:

> By the way of introduction something may here be said about the convictions which brought this Group, with an annual 'Puritan Conference' into being. The Group exists because its organisers believe that historic Reformed theology in general, and the teaching of the great Puritans in particular, does justice to certain neglected Biblical truths and emphases which the church today urgently needs to re-learn.[13]

To return to the early beginnings in 1950, it is salutary to consider how few men fully grasped the doctrines of free grace. David Fountain records that in the 1952 conference Packer showed in his paper on 'Richard Baxter as a Theologian' that Baxter did not hold to the doctrine of particular redemption. In the discussion that followed, the chairman, Dr Lloyd-Jones, pointed out the implications of believing in universal atonement and he was the only one prepared to defend particular redemption. David Fountain says, 'Dr Lloyd-Jones, many years later, reminded me of this occasion when he stood alone on the subject of Particular Redemption.'[14] At the Tyndale Summer School in Theology in Cambridge in July 1953, when Professor John Murray gave an address on definite (as opposed to universal) redemption, there was no senior man present who was prepared to support Murray except Lloyd-Jones. But the situation was about to change.

Dr Lloyd-Jones did all he could to encourage Jim Packer and to support a widening of his influence. As Iain Murray points out in the biography:

Only on one major aspect of the doctrine of salvation did a difference remain between them, namely, on the extent of the atonement. Still sympathetic with Richard Baxter's universal view (and working for a D Phil on Baxter at this time) Packer was silent on the issue at the Cambridge discussion of 1953, already mentioned. But he continued to think and ML-J was delighted at the outcome: 'I will never forget one morning when the Puritan Conference was due to start. Packer came rushing up to me and said, "I am now a complete Calvinist, Doctor!" He had finished with Baxter and turned to Owen. At first I alone was contending for limited atonement.'[15]

In the first twenty years of the Puritan Conference Dr Packer perhaps did more than anyone else to awaken interest in exploring the riches of that heritage. Having absorbed the essence of their thought he articulated it in a fresh way to a generation of students and ministers. For the first five years he contributed two papers to each conference and thereafter one. We see then that from the providential discovery of the writings of a Puritan in the basement of a college in Oxford in 1945 there was to grow a new-found appreciation of those spiritual giants and a movement that was to spread worldwide.

Reflecting on those events after twenty years Packer wrote:

> We did not think of ourselves as setting up a rallying point for a new movement, although in retrospect it now seems that this is what we did; we only knew that the dusty pages of [John] Owen and [Thomas] Goodwin mouldering on the bottom shelves of the OICCU library had become a gold mine to us, and we wanted to share the wealth. So we met and read papers and to help each other by discussion to a firmer grasp of the Puritan profundities.[16]

The papers given by Dr Packer were later gathered in a volume entitled *Among God's Giants: Aspects of Puritan Christianity* (first published in 1991). In the introduction he compared the Puritans to the giant redwood trees in California, some 360 feet tall: 'As redwoods attract the eye because they overtop other trees, so the mature holiness and seasoned fortitude of the great Puritans shine before us as a kind of beacon light, overtopping the stature of the majority of Christians in most eras, and certainly so in this age of crushing urban collectivism.' Their radically God-centred outlook and experimental theology was also captured by Packer in his classic work, *Knowing God*. First published as a volume in 1973, it sold half a million copies within the decade. Through that volume, the Puritan vision of God is continuing to enrich generations of Christians.

Our witness was simple, but we were convinced it was true and urgent, so we spake plainly: the ills of our land and the spiritual poverty of the church arose from the fact that we have offended God and that he has a controversy with us. Our problem is not in empty churches nor in indifferent multitudes but in our own disobedience to the Word of God. We have diluted the gospel by turning it into a man-centred message and we have ceased to make the Scripture the rule of all our practice. In short before everything else, we need to clear out of our lives and out of our pulpits and out of our churches all the things that have caused God to depart from us.

IAIN MURRAY

Iain H. Murray

7.

Iain Murray: 'the new dress'

Another significant stream that flowed into the common influence for the Reformed recovery in the 1950s, and again one closely associated with Dr Lloyd-Jones, was that which came through Iain Murray. He became instrumental in the launching of *The Banner of Truth* magazine in 1955 and the formation of the Banner of Truth Trust in 1957.

Iain H. Murray was born in Lancashire in 1931. His father was a native of Cambuslang, near Glasgow, and his mother's family came from Kirkcudbright in the south-west of Scotland, where Iain briefly went to school at the start of the Second World War. His father, as an engineer, was drawn to the busy port of Liverpool. Iain's secondary education was at King William's College at Castletown on the Isle of Man. The college was a school in the Church of England tradition although Iain's family belonged to the Presbyterian Church of England, and they attended a congregation with a membership of approaching 1,000 people.

Discovering the true gospel

Iain's sister, Jean, was invited by a friend to go to Hildenborough Hall, a Christian conference centre in Kent, founded in 1945 by the evangelist, Tom Rees. Iain was reluctant to go at first but later agreed. There he met a young man of his own age, Eric Alexander. The speaker at the conference was the Rev. Joe Blinco. It was there that Iain first heard the gospel clearly preached and the visit had a lasting effect upon him and his sister. He became a Christian in his final year at King William's College.[1]

Iain was at Hildenborough again in the summer of 1949, as a temporary helper on the staff. One afternoon, while relaxing with other members of staff, the conversation turned to the spiritual blessings of the conference centre and Iain remarked with enthusiasm: 'All the best preachers in the country come here.' There was silence when a young lady calmly corrected him and assured him that he was mistaken. When he asked, 'Who does not come here?' he heard the name of Dr Martyn Lloyd-Jones for the first time. To the further question, 'Why does he not come?' he was given the simple reply, 'He is a Calvinist.'[2]

At this time Iain Murray applied and was accepted as a student for the ministry of the Presbyterian Church of England. On leaving school he was conscripted for National Service and served with the Cameronians (Scottish Rifles) in Malaya, then in the midst of an emergency caused by terrorism. While in the Far East he visited a Christian bookshop in Singapore. He refers in one place to the 'words spoken by a lady missionary to a young soldier in 1951 which sent him to M'Cheyne'. The lady, perceiving a dawning interest in good books, encouraged him to visit, on his return to England, a certain Mr Blatchley, who had a good supply of the best second-hand literature. Later, when he was in London, Iain called at the address given him: '27 Lancefield Street, Kilburn'. When he arrived at the door he was greeted by a gentleman who informed him that it was a few years since Mr Blatchley had 'gone home'. William Blatchley had commenced a ministry in Christian literature in 1887 or 1888, in what was then his parents' home.

The man who greeted Iain Murray was Mr F. J. Hobbs, who had joined Mr Blatchley in 1933. Iain describes the scene:

> On the upper floor of 27 Lancefield Street Mr Hobbs worked as a tailor for a livelihood, while downstairs his Christian ministry took the form of an 'Eldorado' of second-hand Christian literature, filling the wall space and bookcases in every room and intended to meet the needs of all with whom God gave him contact.[3]

It was in the rooms at Lancefield Street that Iain Murray first saw some of the titles that were later to be republished by the Banner of Truth Trust, and he obtained copies of books by such authors as John Owen, John Flavel, Charles Bridges and C. H. Spurgeon. Mr Hobbs gave advice on what to buy. 'Between 1951 and 1954 books from 27 Lancefield Street were used to set us on that road which led first to the magazine and later to the Trust books.'

In 1951 Iain proceeded to Durham University to study for a General Arts degree, where he became involved with the Christian Union. Recalling those days he said:

> It played a far greater part in my active life at university than anything else. Rightly or wrongly the CU was our spiritual home and while we attended church regularly and taught in Sunday School there was no question that the CU and the speakers that came were our main source of help. Most Sunday evenings the CU's evangelistic meetings were crowded out and clearly did good. Of course the CU would be described as pietistic today, but witness was definite and there were, I believe, regular conversions.[4]

Among the speakers at the CU at Durham were some men from north of the Border. One of the more regular visitors was the Rev. R. A. Finlayson, Professor of Systematic Theology at the Free Church College in Edinburgh. It was one of the few theological colleges in the UK that remained committed to the authority of Scripture and the Reformed faith in the first half of the twentieth century. Although he was rooted in the Scottish Highland tradition Finlayson's catholicity of outlook led him into association with Christians of other denominations. His services were eagerly sought after by Christian Unions and other student groups on both sides of the Border. He was destined to have an influence on a number of students, including Iain Murray.

Preparing for the ministry

It was in Durham City, in the summer of 1952, that the library of a former Methodist minister, the Rev. James Shiphardson, became available. He had died a quarter of a century earlier but his daughter had ensured that nothing changed in her father's study. On herself becoming frail, the library became available and the books proved to be a spiritual gold mine to some of the students. Iain procured some thirty or forty choice Puritan volumes, including *The Works of Jonathan Edwards* which he especially prized.[5] The students began to see the evangelical faith in a more historic perspective and this gave them a much deeper interest in doctrine. Iain read the Puritans and discussed what was read with a like-minded group of students: 'None of us had ever been to the Puritan Conference in London, and the resurgence of interest in the Puritans in Durham was not directly linked to what was happening elsewhere.'

In 1954 Iain graduated from Durham and should have proceeded to Westminster College, Cambridge, to study for the ministry of the Presbyterian Church; but providence intervened. His mother had contracted cancer and the ordeal through which she passed was blessed to her conversion. Before that time she had not been used to evangelical teaching. It was then that Iain severed his connection as a student for the ministry of the English Presbyterian Church. There was a disillusionment with the false teaching in which he had been reared. How could he attend a college of a denomination where there was so little of the gospel? He decided on other ways to prepare himself for the Christian ministry. In May 1954 Iain applied to the Free Church College in Edinburgh to be received as a private student. This move was no doubt connected with the friendship of Professor R. A. Finlayson, who was a member of the Senatus. The college required him to sit a Greek entrance exam on a certain date, but this did not materialize because Iain was committed to an army camp at that time.

In the autumn of 1954 Iain Murray proceeded to London and to the Foreign Missions Club in Highbury, principally to be able to sit under the ministry of Dr Martyn Lloyd-Jones. Recalling that time he said:

> I came to know Dr Lloyd-Jones in the early 1950s. He was then at the height of his powers and labours and I was an unknown student for the ministry. Nonetheless he gave me time and counsel as generously as he did to countless other young men.[6]

At the club Iain met with Erroll Hulse and David Fountain, two young men who were to play a part in the recovery of the Calvinistic truths. Erroll was a native of South Africa, and had graduated in architecture at Pretoria University. While at university he was converted during an evangelistic campaign led by the Welsh evangelist, Ivor Powell. He had come with his wife, Lyn, to study extra-murally at London Bible College. At that time Erroll was uncommitted to the Reformed truths; in fact, he described himself as 'a dogmatic Arminian'.

A man who was destined to have an effect on Iain and David was the Rev. Sidney Norton (1907-94) of Oxford. Mr Norton was ministering in a small charge, numbering not more than two dozen people, at St John's, Squitchey Lane, Summerton, Oxford. This congregation had belonged to the Free Church of England, in which Mr Norton had been trained, but by this date it had become an independent Calvinistic church. He got to know about these young men and sought to help them. David Fountain was the first to be strengthened by the teaching and he was followed by Iain.

What Iain Murray regarded as the second main influence giving him the vision was about to unfold. He writes:

> In December 1954 a rich haul of such books from Mr Hobbs, despite their low cost, finished off the savings which were then keeping me in London and sent me back to my parents' home in Cheshire.[7]

His mother died in January 1955. The way forward remained unclear until March 1955 when an invitation came from Mr Norton to join him in the ministry at St John's, Oxford. Iain was by now engaged to Jean Walters, whom he had met at Hildenborough Hall, and after their marriage in April, the young couple moved to Oxford in May 1955.

Discovering the English Reformers

Oxford had seen the great works of God at the time of the Protestant Reformation. The city had been the scene of the martyrdoms of Hugh Latimer and Nicholas Ridley in Queen Mary's cruel reign. Although a monument to these men stood outside Balliol College, people had long forgotten the truth for which these men gave their lives. This prevailing indifference to the Reformation truths in Oxford was the means of deepening concern for the recovery and dissemination of the doctrines of grace.

Iain wrote:

> Close at hand, buildings, libraries and monuments were reminders of those eras when from Oxford's ancient Colleges the doctrines of grace flowed to the whole nation. Those former days of power along with the truths which then moved multitudes all seemed forgotten amidst arid academic theology and a modern evangelicalism which seemed to know nothing of William Tyndale, John Owen or George Whitefield.[8]

Although not a popular preacher, Mr Norton was a man of prayer and faith. He was strong and articulate in his Calvinistic convictions, and he had a burden for the recovery of those truths that made salvation a work of divine grace. This was a burden which Iain shared and the pair looked to the republication of older Christian literature as a means to that end. An old lady in the congregation died and left £40 to Mr Norton. This was put aside for the issue of a magazine. The two men started work and the magazine went to press in July 1955. Iain had planned to name it the *Gospel Banner* but Mr Norton, with the compelling motivation of Psalm 60:3-4, prevailed in naming it *The Banner of Truth*.

After a delay at the printer the first issue appeared in September 1955. In appearance it had no great appeal, for the cover paper was the same as the main text. The six-page editorial was in the joint names of 'Sidney Norton and Ian [a printer's error] Murray'. The message to the reader on the last page was so closely attached to the previous article that it could be easily overlooked and taken for part of it. A section of that message read:

According to the measure in which we are enabled, our desire is to continue to propagate the truth as fully, widely and as often as possible. There are great stores of written treasure, amassed by God's servants in past generations, now lying buried under the dust of time. We wish to unearth this treasure and spread it far and wide on the printed page. We earnestly solicit your prayerful attention.[9]

The magazine was sent to addresses across the UK. The hunger for this teaching was greater than the pair had anticipated. However, resources were so limited that after the first issue there was no income for a second one.

Iain writes:

At this time there was already a longing in our hearts to see the start of a new work of book-publishing. When we visited London in September 1955 to enquire into the costs of printing presses our findings came as a shock.[10]

Further conversation with Dr Lloyd-Jones strengthened the belief that such a thing was possible. The Doctor offered £100 and at the same time encouraged the Westminster Chapel deacons to provide half the sum necessary for the printing of the second issue of *The Banner of Truth* magazine. In the meantime Iain was urged by Dr Lloyd-Jones, given the facilities available at Oxford, to study the writings of the English Reformers with a view to writing a book to demonstrate the Calvinistic convictions of these men.

While continuing his ministry and studies at Oxford, Iain wrote in March 1956 to Dr Lloyd-Jones proposing a meeting with the Rev. W. J. Grier (1902-83) of Belfast and the Rev. G. N. M. Collins (1901-89) of Edinburgh, with the intention of arranging a public meeting to launch a new publishing company for the reissue of Reformed and Puritan classics. The idea did not appeal to the Doctor. He replied:

With regard to the major matter of policy, I am not happy with the suggestion of a public meeting. My idea is that we should first publish books and thus create a constituency ... I feel strongly that the best way is to start very quietly, then to trust God to bless the books that we shall publish. There is all the difference in the world between organising a movement and the sheer weight of truth producing the movement inevitably.[11]

On this matter the Doctor's judgement prevailed and no such meeting took place.

The manuscript on the Calvinistic convictions of the English Reformers was finished by May 1956, by which time it was evident that the slender finances of St John's congregation could no longer support an assistant. The outcome was that in that same month, Dr Lloyd-Jones invited Iain to come as his assistant at Westminster Chapel. The plan was that the assistant would lead a prayer meeting on the Monday evening and a Bible study on the Wednesday. The proposal was approved at a church meeting on 12 July 1956, and Iain took up the position in September 1956. The third issue of *The Banner of Truth* magazine appeared in October 1956, bearing the name of Iain Murray as sole editor, and carrying the address of his new home in London.

Another providential link related to Iain's time in Oxford is worth recording here. It was there in 1955 that he first met Mr Sidney M. Houghton, who was destined to play a significant role in the future work of the Banner of Truth Trust. They were introduced to one another standing in the hallway of Sidney Norton's home. Mr Houghton asked Iain what his personal plans were for the future. 'To serve in the ministry' was Iain's reply, after which a second question was addressed to him: 'And what else?'[12] It seemed almost prophetic! The nature of Mr Houghton's future contribution to the work of the Banner of Truth Trust became apparent when Iain received back from him one of the early issues of the magazine correctly proof-read!

Iain and Jean Murray

Another influence which Mr Houghton had on Iain Murray and the subsequent republishing programme occurred the following year. Iain and Jean left Oxford in July 1956 with a view to going to London. In the interval they paid a five-day visit to the Houghton's home in Rhyl, North Wales, in early August. Mr Houghton had probably one of the largest private collections of books in the country. It filled the extensive loft in the bungalow and two chicken sheds in the garden. By this time Dr Lloyd-Jones had suggested to Iain that the Wednesday evening meeting at Westminster should take the form of an address on church history. With the prospect of this before him Iain received some lessons on the subject from Mr Houghton and left Rhyl with a number of second-hand books that were to be invaluable to him in the months ahead.[13]

Making history live

It was in October 1956 that Iain began the series of addresses on British church history in Westminster Chapel. He would be seen coming into the meeting room with a pile of books, some no doubt from Mr Houghton's collection, others perhaps borrowed from the Evangelical Library. It was soon evident that he had a special gift to 'make history live'. One lady, recalling his account of the Disruption of the Church of Scotland in 1843 and the 200 ministers rising from their seats in St Andrew's Church, Edinburgh, and walking through the streets lined with people to Tanfield Hall, remembers how some of the audience were so moved that they felt like getting up and re-enacting the scene!

In the Wednesday evening gathering was a man who would have stood out in any company. He was six foot four inches in height, with jet black hair and horn-rimmed spectacles. He listened with rapt attention to Iain's lectures on the Reformers and the Puritans. Jack Cullum (1910-1971), like his father before him, was a highly successful acoustic engineer. For the first thirty years of his working life, the pursuit of success in business was the absorbing interest of his life. His business flourished due to several inventions, but especially one during the Second World War, of mufflers to reduce the noise of jet aircraft when they were being tested on the ground. A nominal Methodist, he had long ceased attending church and his marriage was 'on the rocks'. While on a business trip to the USA in 1955, and crossing on the Queen Elizabeth, he sat at the dining table with a couple who were earnest Christians, Stanley and Kathleen Clark. Stanley was the manager of Barclays Bank in Jerusalem. Their witness to him was followed by an invitation to their home in Jerusalem where, on Christmas Day 1955, Mr Cullum found assurance of salvation. Not being able to find soul-satisfying preaching in his former denomination in North London, Jack Cullum was advised to attend the ministry of Dr Lloyd-Jones at Westminster Chapel.

After being thrilled by the truths that now inspired his soul, it was clear that Mr Cullum wished to do something to further the knowledge of them. He invited Iain and Jean Murray to his home in Highgate. As they walked together on Hampstead

Heath on 26 January 1957 Cullum put a question to Iain: 'Why is it that all the history and teaching of the English Reformers and Puritans is so little known today?'[14] On hearing of the long period during which the works of these men had been unavailable through booksellers, Iain says that he had no idea that he was speaking to someone whom God was calling to support their re-publication. Dr Lloyd-Jones had some reservations about proceeding with such a venture but by mid-March 1957 plans were developed for the establishment of a charitable trust. The trust deeds of the Banner of Truth Trust were formally signed on 22 July 1957.

Launching the books

At its inception the trust's editorial work operated from a basement room in Iain Murray's home in St John's Wood, while stock was held 'in a room no bigger than a store cupboard', temporarily loaned for the purpose in Westminster Chapel. The first books to be reprinted carried the address of Mr Cullum's business: '58-59 Highgate West Hill, London N6'. 'By November ten books were at the printers and before Christmas the first two volumes of Watson's *Body of Divinity* and Burrowes on *The Song of Solomon* were available.' In February 1958 the ground floor of the building at 78 Chiltern Street was leased from St Paul's Church, Portman Square, for the modest sum of £450 per annum. Already installed on the top floor of the building was the Evangelical Library, which had made a significant contribution to the awakening of interest in the Calvinistic heritage. The work began in Chiltern Street 'with a staff of three seated on parcels fresh from the printers and using as a table four old benches left behind by the former occupants'.

Iain was joined in the work of the trust by his friend from Durham Christian Union days, Don Elcoat. Others also came

The beginnings of the work at 78 Chiltern St, 1958

forward to help. Erroll Hulse, his companion at the Foreign Missions Club, influenced by the lectures of Dr Ernest Kevan, the preaching of Dr Lloyd-Jones and the friendship of Iain Murray, had changed his doctrinal views: 'It was reading the recently published commentary by Robert Haldane on Romans in five volumes (published by Jay Green) that cured me completely of Arminianism. By the end of Romans chapter three I was a firm five point Calvinist.'[15] In 1957 he left architecture to take up a full-time job as manager at the trust.

When the trust first began, it was the opinion in the world of religious publishing that a programme so heavily dependent on 'out-of-date' authors could not possibly succeed. For decades there had been little or no demand for Puritan books in the second-hand book market and it was reasonable to suppose that nothing — not even low prices or attractive jackets — could make people buy books which they did not want. What the religious world did not reckon with was the hunger that had been created in Christian hearts. Dr Robert Oliver recalls the occasion when Dr Lloyd-Jones gave a recommendation of the newly reprinted *A Body of Divinity* by Thomas Watson at his Friday evening Bible study in early January 1958. He announced that copies were available in the chapel book room. As Robert made his way to the book room he discovered a queue of people stretching from the shop all along the courtyard. The initial supply quickly ran out and Iain Murray had to come to the rescue with a packet from the stockroom.

The pessimism and doubt that had greeted the commencement of the venture were quickly dispelled. The sales of the new titles exceeded expectations. Erroll Hulse recalls what happened with one bookshop:

> One of the first books to be published by the Banner was *A Body of Divinity* by Thomas Watson. I took six copies to the then leading bookshop in the West End of London in Wigmore Street. Edward England was the manager. He kindly assured me that this old-fashioned book would not sell. I assured him that if he could not sell the six copies we would take them back. Reluctantly he took the books. About three days later he phoned to order another twelve copies! And not too long after that twenty-four copies.[16]

Sales figures began to be recorded in February 1958. By the end of that year *A Body of Divinity* by Thomas Watson had sold 2,519 copies. *The Select Sermons of George Whitefield* came a close second with 2,319 copies. By the end of 1958 fourteen titles were in print and the total sales amounted to 19,834. By the close of 1960 the sales of *A Body of Divinity* had reached a total of 5,354. The books were selling through the usual outlets. It was not long before the Scripture Union Bookshop in Wigmore Street, which Erroll referred to, had a large window display

Window display of Banner titles at SU Bookshop, Wigmore Street, 1958

devoted entirely to the new Banner titles, with a framed picture of the Westminster Assembly at the centre of it.

Love for the doctrines contained in the reprints began to influence students and young people. Peter Golding, who had been converted under the preaching of Dr Lloyd-Jones and was a student at London Bible College, wrote to Iain Murray:

> Although comparatively young in the faith I am coming more and more to see the relevance and absolute necessity of the doctrines of sin and grace which you are drawing attention to. I have put a list of Banner of Truth publications on our common room notice board and have already sold three copies of Watson's work... It is quite incredible the way in which antipathy is being shown towards truths which humble man and exalt God.[17]

Peter began helping on a voluntary basis and after finishing his college course became the accountant in the trust offices, until he received a call to Hayes Town Chapel.

Humphrey Mildred was another student who became enthusiastic about the Banner work and began helping while at London Bible College. After a short time as assistant to the Rev. David Fountain in Southampton, Humphrey felt that he wished to devote himself fully to the promotion of the Banner work and began full-time work there in 1959, eventually becoming the production manager. It was an honour for me to be invited to join the editorial department as assistant to Iain Murray in June 1960. Some of the students and others who helped in the first year or two went on to be influential in the Reformed cause — Robin Bird, Paul Brown, Alan Gibson, Clive Tyler, John Legg, Paul Helm, Gordon Hawkins, and Ron and Anne Davies — to name a few.

The ability to make church history live and inspire enthusiasm in others which Iain displayed in his lectures at Westminster

Staff at the Banner of Truth Trust, 1962

Erroll Hulse, Humphrey Mildred and John J. Murray in centre of group

Chapel was now exercised in the wider literary field. It is not without significance that the first volume from Iain's pen was *The Forgotten Spurgeon.* It was as if the Spurgeon prophecy had been fulfilled to the letter:

> I am quite willing to be eaten by dogs for the next fifty years but the more distant future shall vindicate me.

The years of distortion were at an end and Spurgeon in his life and writings was opened to a new generation. His *Commenting and Commentaries* led to treasured expositions from the past being brought to light. Puritan writings appeared in 'new dress'.

There are so many temptations to allow the claims of truth to become secondary. Mental laziness is one of these temptations. We have become accustomed to a certain pattern of thought and conduct. It may be surrounded by the halo of sanctity derived from an established family, social or ecclesiastical tradition, and we are not willing to bring this pattern or conviction to the test of these criteria which the truth demands. Or perhaps after persuasion to the contrary by the evidence of truth, we are not willing to let truth have its way, just because it means a breach with the convenient and the conventional.

JOHN MURRAY

Professor John Murray

8.
John Murray: 'the old school piety'

The movement that led to 'the recovery of the vision' in the 1950s was largely confined to England and Wales. This is perhaps another indication of the crucial role played by Dr D. Martyn Lloyd-Jones, that native Welshman who ministered most of his life in England. That does not mean to say there were not connections and influences that affected Northern Ireland and Scotland. The witness of the Rev. W. J. Grier and the Irish Evangelical Church, with the widespread contribution of the Evangelical Bookshop, has already been noted.

There were also connections with the Scottish scene. Dr Lloyd-Jones was a welcome preacher in Scotland. As early as 1939 he preached at a week of meetings in the Usher Hall in Edinburgh and in 1942 gave a series of lectures at the Free Church College. He had close associations with Daniel Lamont, Principal John MacLeod and G. N. M. Collins. Iain Murray, with his Scottish lineage, began to glean from the riches of the Scottish Reformed heritage. His early connections were with men like Eric Alexander and Professor R. A. Finlayson. It would be true to say that due to the strength of the Confessional Churches in Scotland, the Reformed vision had not been lost to the same extent as it had been in England. Nevertheless, with the increasing popularity of modern evangelistic methods there appeared to be a weakening of confidence in the Reformed message.[1]

In the late 1950s, after I came to appreciate the writings of A. W. Pink, reprints of the Sovereign Grace Book Club and *The Banner of Truth* magazine, I made an effort to awaken more interest in the resurgence of these truths by launching in 1959 a quarterly magazine entitled *Eternal Truth.* A great welcome was given to this venture by the Rev. Kenneth A. MacRae (1883-1964), minister of the Free Church of Scotland congregation in Stornoway.[2] He ordered 150 copies immediately. Mr MacRae was contending that there was a drift in doctrinal commitment in the church in Scotland and longed and prayed for the dawn of 'a new day'. A man who was destined to be part of the answer to that prayer was at that time expounding the glories of the Reformed faith on the other side of the Atlantic. He was a man who throughout his life epitomized all that was best in the old Scottish Reformed heritage.

John Murray, a Free Presbyterian by birth, had left Scotland's shores in 1929 to teach at Princeton Theological Seminary and, for the rest of his working life, at Westminster Theological Seminary. Born one year before Dr Lloyd-Jones there was a similarity in the way of providence with them. The initial loss to Wales and Scotland by their calls elsewhere was compensated by a greater influence on the United Kingdom as a whole and indeed the rest of the world. John Murray was to be linked in that recovery, not only with Dr Lloyd-Jones but with his fellow student at Princeton, the Rev. W. J. Grier and with the Rev. Kenneth A. MacRae.

Highland heritage

John Murray's roots were in the Highlands of Scotland. He was born on 14 October 1898 in Badbea, in the parish of Creich, in the county of Sutherland. The nearest village was Bonar Bridge. The family home on the shores of Loch Migdale was surrounded by some of the most delightful scenery in the Highlands. His parents were Alexander (Sandy) and Catherine Murray and John was the youngest of a family of six sons and two daughters. The croft, consisting of thirty acres of arable land surrounding the home, was the mainstay of the family income. In

John Murray's home at Badbea, taken 2005

the year of John's birth an event occurred which relieved some of the poverty for the people of the district. Andrew Carnegie returned from the United States, where he made his fortune in steel. He bought Skibo Castle, near Dornoch, and embarked on erecting new wings to the building. He also set about building new roads on the extensive Skibo estate. Sandy Murray was contracted by Carnegie for road-making, fencing and ditching. Most of the time he had to employ men but it is said that he always paid them the same rate as himself.

Although the home at Badbea was overcrowded and the family were poor, its great adornments were godliness and prayer. The parish of Creich had been powerfully affected by the gospel. Under the ministry of George Rainy (1771-1810) it is said that 'over 100 men could openly testify to a personal work of grace and give a reason for the hope that was in them.'[3] When a Moderate (non-evangelical) minister was imposed on the parish in 1811, the congregation left the building and met on the shores of Loch Migdale, under a great rock. The legislation that permitted the imposition of a minister on an unwilling people led ultimately to the Disruption of 1843 and the formation of the Free Church of Scotland. The minister of the Creich parish after 1843 was the Rev. Dr Gustavus Aird, and it was under his ministry that Sandy Murray became an elder at the early age of twenty-seven.

The Higher Critical views that began to infiltrate the colleges of the Free Church of Scotland in the 1870s meant that another 'disruption' of the church became increasingly likely. The weakening in commitment to the *Westminster Confession of Faith*, culminating in the Declaratory Act of 1892, led to two Highland ministers breaking away from the Free Church and forming the Free Presbyterian Church in 1893. Sandy Murray, in spite of his love for his minister, Dr Aird, felt he could not remain in the Free Church and in 1895 joined the new church. It was therefore in that denomination that the infant John Murray was baptized in the spring of 1899.

As a child growing up in that godly home John Murray imbibed true piety. Every morning and evening there was family worship, with psalm singing, Scripture reading and prayer. The Sabbath day, after special preparations on Saturday, was observed with family worship, public worship and private spiritual exercises, like catechism instruction and the reading of good books. The twice-yearly Communion season, lasting five days, brought godly folk from neighbouring parishes to participate. Badbea, like other homes, would be a centre of hospitality and fellowship during the five days.

John Murray was moulded by the example of his father in particular. He could say of him:

I never witnessed a greater intensity of spiritual exercise of soul in any other person. His very body moved in sympathy with the inner man.[4]

Close as he was later to come to some of the godly theologians of Princeton and Westminster Seminaries, he always maintained that the man who had the greatest influence on him was his father.

There is not much on record of John Murray's childhood years. After his primary education at the local Bonar Bridge School, he moved on to Dornoch Academy. This meant that he had to cycle twelve miles from his home on the Monday morning, live in lodgings for four nights, and cycle back home on the Friday afternoon. After gaining his 'Highers' at the academy he was called up for military service in the First World War, serving with the Black Watch in France. Eight months after enlisting, he was involved in an Allied advance. While leading his men, and in the act of firing his rifle, he was hit in the right eye by shrapnel. He was moved to a hospital in England where his eye was removed to be replaced by one of glass.

Studying for the ministry

On 10 December 1918 he was discharged from the army and returned to Badbea. His preservation was the fulfilment of an assurance that Sandy Murray had been given at his son's baptism from Psalm 92:13-14: 'They shall still bring forth fruit in old age.' Donald and Thomas, two other sons from that home, had been lost in the war. Having an intimacy with the Lord so typical of many Highland worthies, when Tommy left Ardgay railway station for the Dardanelles Sandy Murray said, 'I'll never see you again.' In the autumn of 1919 John entered the University of Glasgow. In the hope that less strain would be placed on his eyesight, his arts course was extended over four years. He graduated MA on 20 June 1923.

By the time he graduated he was a communicant member of the Free Presbyterian Church of Scotland. He was convinced that God was calling him to the ministry. He preached his first sermon in Stratherrick, Inverness-shire in 1922 upon the words, 'His name shall be called Wonderful' (Isaiah 9:6). Examined by the Kirk Session of his home congregation in Creich he was recommended to the Northern Presbytery as a candidate for the ministry. The training scheme operated by his church was for men in pastoral charges to act as tutors to prepare students for the ministry. The tutor to whom John Murray went, in the autumn of 1923, was the Rev. Donald Beaton, in Wick, Caithness. John showed such promise in his studies that before his first year was over, it was agreed that he should proceed to Princeton Theological Seminary in the USA for his final two years, to be ready to serve as a future theological tutor in his own church.

At the beginning of the twentieth century the name of Princeton Theological Seminary was regarded even in the Highlands of Scotland as a place of pure orthodoxy and piety. It had been founded in 1812 to provide ministerial training for Presbyterians. The first professor was Archibald Alexander and he was followed by such renowned theologians as Charles Hodge, A. A. Hodge and B. B. Warfield. Princeton theologians advocated Reformed Confessionalism. In his famous remark that 'a new idea never originated in this Seminary', Charles Hodge epitomized Princeton's claim to be merely a bearer of an unbroken and unaltered Calvinism. Books written by Archibald Alexander and Charles Hodge were read and appreciated in Christian homes in the Highlands.

Like all immigrants arriving in the USA at that time John Murray had to pass through the twenty-seven-acre Ellis Isle. He had no work permit and it appears that he did not have any papers on him linking him to Princeton Theological Seminary. He was detained there for two or three days until the seminary was contacted and one of its staff was sent to collect him. He joined the other 225 students commencing the one hundred and thirteenth session of the seminary. With him among the student body was the Rev. W. J. Grier from Northern Ireland, a year his senior, and a man whose life was destined to be intertwined with John Murray's at a later date.

Although unknown to Murray at the time he arrived there, differences were beginning to surface in Princeton Seminary with regard to the attitude to be taken on the new liberal views appearing in the Presbyterian Church in the USA. A turning point as far as the seminary was concerned was the death of the great Benjamin B. Warfield in 1921. When the event occurred J. Gresham Machen wrote these words to his mother: 'It seemed to me that the old Princeton — a great institution as it was — died when Dr Warfield was carried out.'[5] There were good men on the faculty, including Caspar Wistar Hodge, Geerhardus Vos, Robert Dick Wilson, O. T. Allis and J. Gresham Machen. His time as a student at the seminary was destined to have a profound influence on Murray. All the professors had an effect on him, but Geerhardus Vos was his great discovery and inspiration.

It was while studying at Princeton Seminary that John Murray was employed to preach in the congregations of the Free Presbyterian Church of Scotland that had been formed among Scottish emigrants to North America. The minister of one of those congregations was the Rev. William Matheson of Chesley in Ontario. He was engaged at that time in a difference with the church at home over the use of public transport for churchgoing on Sundays. The church ruled that members who used 'street cars' to attend the house of God would be debarred from sitting at the Lord's Table. Matheson, while not himself agreeing with the use of public transport on the Lord's Day, felt that it was wrong to deny privileges to those who did this. His views were later expressed in the publication *May Sabbath-Keeping Prevent Church-Going*.[6] John Murray had come to a similar conviction and when it became known that his sympathies were with the position taken by Mr Matheson, he lost favour with the leaders of the FP Church.

Call to Princeton and Westminster

At this stage, not knowing where his future ministry lay, Murray, who had won a Gelston-Winthrop Fellowship at Princeton, took up further study at New College, Edinburgh University. While engaged in that pursuit he received an invitation from Professor Caspar Wistar Hodge to assist him in the Systematic Theology department at Princeton Seminary. He replied by cable. A student in the same home recalls seeing Murray going out of the house after midnight to get the cheap cable rate! A difficulty arose when it was discovered that the US Consulate in Edinburgh had their quota of visas filled for the next ten years. Someone suggested to him that he try the US Consulate in Glasgow, and he got one immediately.

It was a changed Princeton to which John Murray returned in September 1929, as it was now under the authority of the General Assembly of the Presbyterian Church in the USA. In 1928 that body determined to reorganize the seminary to make it represent a broad range of opinion in the church, including liberalism. Murray had wisely committed himself to only one year. Practically nothing is known of his teaching year at Princeton. The remark of his friend Ned B. Stonehouse that 'he did not find the atmosphere in the reorganized Princeton congenial' is understandable.

The decision of the General Assembly led to three of Princeton's leading professors — Oswald T. Allis, Robert Dick Wilson and J. Gresham Machen — resigning, followed by the young Cornelius

Library room of WTS, 1528 Pine St, Philadelphia, its first location

van Til. This left the Princeton faculty with only two upholders of the old theology — Caspar Wistar Hodge and Geerhardus Vos; William B. Greene had died in 1928. In July 1929 the men who resigned from Princeton founded Westminster Theological Seminary, to continue the old Princeton ethos. The new seminary opened on 25 September, with fifty students. Murray kept in touch with J. Gresham Machen, who in March 1930 arranged for Murray to receive a copy of his new book, *The Virgin Birth of Christ.* A few months later Machen approached Murray with a request that was to have far-reaching consequences for him and for the Reformed world. It was a letter, dated 25 June 1930, inviting him to take the vacant place in the Systematic Theology department of Westminster Theological Seminary.

Murray could not give a response until the matter of his relation to the Free Presbyterian Church had been finalized. In May

1930 the synod of the church decreed that on the question of 'travelling by hired conveyances to church on Sabbath', if 'Murray does not withdraw the opposition by 30 October he will no longer be considered as a student of this Church'. So on 15 September 1930 he wrote a letter to Dr Machen officially accepting the position of 'Instructor' in Westminster Theological Seminary.

Reformed resurgence in England

When Murray came on visits to his family home in the 1930s the pulpits of the Free Presbyterian Church were not open to him. He remained a member of the congregation in Creich and would attend the services there with the rest of the family. However, after his ordination in the Orthodox Presbyterian Church in 1937, membership ceased, and on his visits home following World War Two it was in public halls, under no denominational auspices, that he preached. Also at that time his name was scarcely known among evangelicals in England. The prevailing ethos of English evangelicalism (a modified form of the Fundamentalist ethos of America) and that of John Murray were alien to each other. However, his visits to England at that time coincided with the resurgence of interest in the Reformed faith. It was inevitable that those who had recently felt the power of the doctrines of grace should gravitate to him. John Murray, then in his full spiritual maturity, brought powerful corroboration and gave further momentum to the thinking that was bringing about a new departure in English evangelicalism.

Professor Murray's first contact with the emerging Reformed movement was when he visited the Evangelical Library, recently moved from Beddington, Surrey, to Kensington, London, in the summer of 1945. He met a kindred spirit there in the Rev. E. J. Poole-Connor and the two book enthusiasts went round the shelves together examining the treasures. He was home again in 1948, but it was during his summer vacation in 1953 that he fulfilled a number of speaking engagements in the United Kingdom. The first was in June when Dr Lloyd-Jones, as President of the Evangelical Library, invited him to give the Annual Library Lecture on 'Reformation Principles'. On 6 July of the same year he gave the Tyndale Biblical Theology Lecture in Selwyn College, Cambridge, under the auspices of the Tyndale Fellowship for Biblical Research. The subject was 'The Covenant of Grace' and it was published in a booklet the following year by Tyndale Press.[7]

The lecture was delivered at the time when the Summer School for theological students was meeting in Cambridge. He gave a paper at the school on 'Limited atonement'. Edwin King, who was present as a student, captures the occasion:

> His paper on 'Limited atonement' was a classic, and a child could have followed it. He was obviously in his element, and in my opinion I have never heard anyone who could better him on the theme. Of course, as soon as he had finished, the sniping commenced. Apart from the chairman (Dr Lloyd-Jones) there were few there who were not concerned to defend a universal atonement. Not without considerable excitement it was urged that Murray's belief would inhibit evangelism; that it would kill enthusiasm for witness and concern for the lost! After listening quietly to such objections, John Murray rose to his feet, moved in front of the table, and began to pace up and down the centre aisle between the chairs on which we were sitting. His eyes gleamed, and I could tell he had been stirred by the carnality of it all. In his dark sombre clothes and sallow appearance he was, to me, a most moving sight. Then, very deliberately and slowly, he began: 'I can honestly say I have never heard the gospel

preached more sweetly and savingly to sinners, nor with more saving power, than it was when I heard it as a boy up in...' I could not catch the name of the place, but I knew he was referring to the Highlands of Scotland. The meeting was at once sobered down, and he then began to reminisce about the old preachers — how passionately they held to each of the 'five points' and how God had owned their ministries to the quickening and awakening of sinners.[8]

From Cambridge he moved on to attend the meetings of the Reformed Ecumenical Synod in Edinburgh. After that, he fulfilled some speaking engagements in his native Sutherland. Dr Ae. D. MacLeod, a son of the Rev. Principal John MacLeod, and Mr Alexander Murray, a local elder, arranged for Professor Murray to preach in the Carnegie Hall, Dornoch, at 8 o'clock on Sunday 23 August, after the regular services of the day. His text was John 6:37: 'All that the Father giveth shall come to me and he that cometh to me I will in no wise cast out.' The hall was packed to capacity. I was then in my late teens and under soul concern. As I sat on the floor in the front row only a foot or two away from the preacher I began to tremble. Never had I heard the truth preached with such majesty, eloquence and passion!

In the academic year 1955-56 Professor Murray had been given 'sabbatical leave' to work on his *magnum opus,* the commentary on the Epistle to the Romans. We note that his Atlantic crossing in November was his twenty-second. He spent some time in libraries in Edinburgh and Glasgow for research on Romans. His return passage was on 12 April, and the time before the start of the next academic year was spent on preparing the commentary on Romans. The next time Murray was in the UK was in June 1958 to give the Campbell Morgan Bible Lecture at Westminster Chapel on 'The Heavenly High Priestly activity of Christ'.

Banner work and the Leicester Conference

When the first announcement of the publications work which the Banner of Truth Trust planned to undertake was made, indebtedness was expressed to three men — Dr D. M. Lloyd-Jones, Rev. W. J. Grier and Professor John Murray. As we have seen, W. J. Grier was the chief instrument through the Evangelical Bookshop in Belfast of distributing Reformed books in the UK some years before the Reformed recovery had gained momentum. In Grier and Murray we had two men of confessional Presbyterian background, and moulded by the influence of Princeton Theological Seminary, coming together for this 'new dawn'. It is also significant that the first two Banner titles for which Murray wrote recommendations were *Princeton Sermons* by Charles Hodge and *Jonathan Edwards' Select Works.*

Through his identification with the Banner of Truth Trust work, Professor Murray developed a much closer connection with the church situation in England and this gave further momentum to the recovery of Reformed truth. Already the conviction was growing that the absence of an appreciation of the majesty of God and the lack of conviction of sin in evangelicalism were signs of the need for true revival. As was the case in previous history, the lack was first evident in the message from the pulpit. The matter had been addressed by Professor Murray in speaking to the Alumni of Westminster Theological Seminary on 19 February 1952 on 'Some Necessary Emphases in Preaching'. The first emphasis he dealt with was 'The ministry of judgement':

> What I have observed as conspicuously minimal in the preaching of evangelical and even Reformed churches is the proclamation of the demands and sanctions of the law of God. To put it bluntly, it is the lack of the enunciation with power and earnestness and passion of the demands and terrors of God's law.[9]

Professor Murray saw that a change was needed in the pulpit. There must be a restoration of true preaching. A man who shared this concern was the Rev. J. Marcellus Kik, a trustee of Westminster Theological Seminary. This whole problem was discussed with Mr Kik when he was present at the trust headquarters in London in 1961. As a result he carried back to Professor Murray in Philadelphia a proposal that a conference should be held for ministers the following year (1962) in the United Kingdom, concentrating specifically on the need for a renewal of preaching. Other men were consulted about this. Among them were the Rev. W. J. Grier of Belfast and the Rev. Kenneth MacRae of Stornoway.

As has been noted already, Mr MacRae was conscious of a drift that was taking place in the church in Scotland and even, he feared, within his own denomination. He longed and prayed for a recovery of truth and godliness and believed that 'the tide will turn'. The advent of *The Banner of Truth* magazine in 1955 was an encouragement to him and he personally ordered quantities of between 150 and 200 copies. It was with the prospect of helping forward this new work that he accepted the invitation to speak at the 1962 Ministers' Conference. Although then in his seventy-ninth year he made the long journey from the Isle of Lewis to undertake what was his first and last preaching engagements in England. As well as speaking at the Leicester Conference, he took the Communion services in the Free Church of Scotland congregation in London and preached at Grove Chapel, London, where Iain Murray had been inducted as minister the previous year.

It was in this way that the Lord in his providence brought together men from different countries, but in the Reformed tradition, to address the need for the restoration of true preaching. A venue for the conference was found through the good offices of the Rev. Sidney Lawrence, minister of Knighton Evangelical Church, Leicester — at College Hall on the campus

John Murray: 'the old school piety'

First Leicester Ministers' Conference, July 1962

Front centre: Kenneth MacRae, John Murray, W. J. Grier

of Leicester University. W. J. Grier opened the conference with an address on 'Preaching and the present age' and closed with 'The preacher and prayer.' Iain Murray dealt with 'Preaching in England in the past.' Professor Murray gave three addresses on 'Preaching and 1) Scripture; 2) Sanctification; 3) Judgement.' The Rev. Kenneth MacRae's subjects were 'Teaching essential to Evangelical preaching' and 'The danger of compromise in preaching.'

Forty men attended the first conference, of which thirty were ministers in pastoral charges. The majority came from England but there were twelve from Scotland and three from Northern Ireland. Wales was not represented. As a member of the Banner of Truth staff I was appointed secretary of the conference and duly relieved attendees of the princely sum of £3, for full board over three days. If a minister's travel expenses amounted to more than £1, a claim for assistance could be made.

143

The discussions at the conference centred around the growing interest in Reformed truth and the desirability of united action on the part of those who held to the doctrines of free grace. Professor Murray spoke very movingly about what he had heard and witnessed that day as being the answer to prayer and the fulfilment of a vision he had for the restoration of the Reformation doctrines in the United Kingdom. Many felt that a new day had indeed dawned.

Back in Stornoway after the conference, the seventy-eight-year-old Mr MacRae, addressing the people of his congregation on 'The present prospects of the Reformed faith', reported that he had seen in England 'a little cloud like a man's hand' (1 Kings 18:44). In further reflecting on the conference he wrote to a friend:

> The earnestness and spiritual unity of those young fellows who gathered at Leicester was for me a real tonic and encouraged me greatly. So far, the movement towards the Reformed Faith may be weak and largely unorganised, but that there is such a movement cannot be questioned, and in it, by God's grace, there are tremendous possibilities. Worm Jacob may yet thresh the mountains. May the Lord grant it so![10]

There was no conference arranged in 1963. Such was the growing appreciation of the influence of Professor Murray that the time of the conference was arranged to suit his availability. The next one was held in July 1964, when Murray spoke on the 'Nature, unity and government of the church'. Dr Lloyd-Jones was present for the first time. The issues raised by Professor Murray were new to many of the men present and, although discussions took place, there was no consensus. More thought had to be given to the matter. The addresses by John Murray were printed in pamphlet form. A selection of Reformed and

Puritan documents dealing with church issues was published under the title *The Reformation of the Church* in time for the next conference which was held in April 1965. Of this conference Murray said,

> I was not so happy about the Conference as on other occasions. I was at odds with what appeared to be the prevailing sentiment, but I had the support of my best friends, including Iain Murray and others who I esteem most highly.[11]

The Ministers' Conference did not meet in 1966, but in the following year a fresh start was made with the emphasis on the life and work of the minister. The main speaker was a new figure to the UK scene, the Rev. Albert Martin, but one highly commended as a preacher by Professor John Murray. Mr Martin was back the following year when he shared the teaching with Professor John Murray at a School in Theology held in London in 1968. It was October 1978 before a similar conference began in the USA — at Atlanta in Georgia, with John de Witt, Al Martin and Walt Chantry as the main speakers.

His contribution

John Murray manifested in his life and teaching all that was best in the Highland piety and in the piety and theology of 'old Princeton', which was carried on into Westminster Theological Seminary. He did this for Westminster and the Reformed cause in the USA almost single-handedly after the death of J. Gresham Machen. David Wells says of Charles Hodge, one of Murray's predecessors: 'We find his work an almost classic realization of the kneeling as opposed to the sitting theologian. He had seen the grace and glory of God and in his Systematic Theology he turns to the world to explain his vision.' With John Murray there was no such thing as a purely academic study of theology. William Perkins described theology 'as the science of living blessedly for ever.' Theological understanding and practical piety are inseparable. This is what Professor Murray demonstrated in his life and teaching. This is what he sought to preserve in an age when the two were being put asunder in the church by modern scholarship.

To the students at Westminster Seminary and to the Reformed world in general Professor Murray demonstrated that the Reformed faith is purely and simply the teaching of Scripture. 'Thus he presented Reformed doctrine in the most persuasive way to Christian minds and hearts.' If Professor Murray had remained within the denomination he was nurtured in, the fear of a breach with traditional views might have restricted his theological research. As it turned out, he worked at the cutting edge of theological scholarship, read the works of liberal theologians and used all the tools of modern biblical studies to articulate the Reformed faith in his own day. It was his theological erudition that made him the finest Reformed theologian of the twentieth century and gave Westminster Seminary a status that was second to none in the Reformed world.[12]

For the Reformed movement in the United Kingdom in general and for the Banner of Truth Trust in particular to have had the privilege of his example and counsel in the formative days of the recovery of the Reformed vision was an inestimable blessing. To be the custodians of his writings ensures that his legacy will be blessed to coming generations.

Faith imbued with zeal for the honour of Christ and the glory of God will have no sympathy with the defeatism which is, after all, but disguised fatalism. He who is head over all things is head over all things to his body the church. He has all authority in heaven and in earth. And he is the Lord of the Spirit. Implicit in the prayer he taught his disciples to pray, 'thy will be done as in heaven so in earth', is the prayer that the whole earth should be filled with his praise. Nothing less is the measure of the believer's desire. 'And blessed be his glorious name for ever; and let the whole earth be filled with his glory'.

JOHN MURRAY

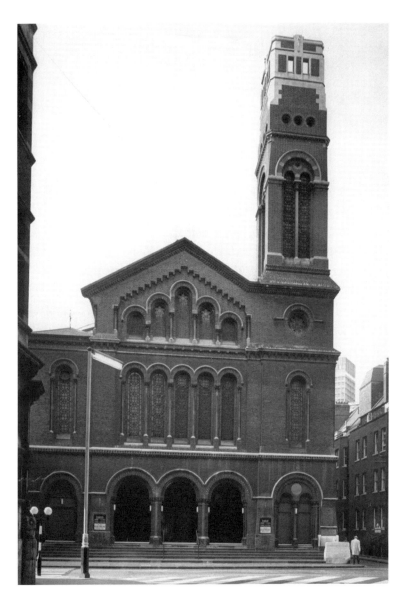

Westminster Chapel, London

9.
Maintaining the vision

When we look back on the change that took place in the middle of the twentieth century we cannot but believe that it was 'a work wrought of God'. It is important to look at the wider picture and to see the workings of the Spirit of God at different times in preparation for the flowering of the work. One is struck by the spontaneity with which certain events unfolded — the forming of the evangelical student witness in the universities in 1919, the call of Dr Lloyd-Jones into the ministry in South Wales, the work of the Spirit among students in North Wales that gave birth to the Evangelical Movement of Wales, and the origins of the Puritan Conference. And all this took place before a Puritan reprint had appeared!

It is true to say that the recovery of the Reformed vision could not be put down to any one agency. A writer in *Crusade* magazine in 1977 spoke of 'the revival of Reformed theology' as 'sparked off largely by the setting up of the Banner of Truth Trust which flooded the market with shelves of inexpensive reprints of Puritan classics'. Iain Murray was quick to counter this when he wrote:

But the truth is that in God's purposes a change in the spiritual climate was coming in the 1950s — there was a sound of a going in the tops of the mulberry trees — and the Trust, far from being the cause of the change, was but one of the agencies raised up to meet the need of a spiritual hunger in many lives and churches.[1]

As we have sought to show in these pages the most influential human agency in bringing the work forward was Dr Martyn Lloyd-Jones and his ministry at Westminster Chapel. Iain Murray recalls what it was like in those days:

By the late 1950s there were hundreds of people, and notably young people, whose thinking and theology had been permanently changed through the pulpit of Westminster Chapel. For a few years their number seemed to be constantly multiplying. It was to a degree reminiscent of the days when John Knox could write of God 'raining men from heaven', or when Thomas Goodwin could speak of the Gospel being at 'full-tide' among students at Cambridge. Swelling numbers was a characteristic of these years.[2]

What those days meant to some is well articulated by Maurice Roberts, who succeeded Iain Murray as Editor of *The Banner of Truth* magazine in 1988. In penning a personal tribute to Mr Murray on the occasion of his retirement as Editorial Director of the trust in 1996, he recalled their early acquaintance. He said that he first heard of Westminster Chapel, Dr Lloyd-Jones and Iain Murray from a fellow student at Durham University. In 1957 on an 'unplanned' stopover in London he was able to attend Westminster Chapel and listened to Mr Murray lead the Sunday afternoon Bible study. At that time the names of Spurgeon, Ryle, Calvin and Owen were all new to him. In 1959 he joined his Christian Union friends for a conference in the Lake District at which Iain Murray spoke on 'The Holiness of God'. His reaction was: 'I gazed on a world of truth such as I had not entered before.'

Recalling the effect of the early Banner titles on him he wrote:

> Many, many readers will know what I mean when I say that the 1960s were years of buying virtually every Banner book as it came out and reading it greedily. The Bible in consequence became a new book to us. Theology became more precious than daily food. It was the frame of reference for all our thinking and living. The choice of our church, the principles of our worship, the habits of a lifetime — all these and similar things were being shaped and moulded.[3]

Expecting revival

In those early days of the recovery we had high hopes that the outcome would be a revival of true religion. Dr Lloyd-Jones believed that the greatest need of the church, namely a true revival, was closely related to a recovery of the Calvinistic truths. He had prayed and worked for that stronger doctrinal position in the church and he expected something great to follow. On a visit to the Banner offices on 29 May 1963 he shared the view with Erroll Hulse that 'the present Reformed awakening' is probably the preparation for revival. He agreed that there were 'about seventy truly Reformed preachers in England and five times that number were soundly evangelical'.[4]

Some three years earlier, in writing the introduction to the first bound edition of *The Banner of Truth* magazine, Iain Murray sought to weigh up the prospects:

The Holy Spirit is now doing a work in spreading the light of truth in the minds of a number of Christ's servants; it may be that he is but strengthening a remnant who will have to stand fast, like Noah and Jeremiah, through a flood of apostasy, sin and judgement; or it may be that this is but a step to a further blessing and that he is now preparing ambassadors who amidst of a general outpouring of the Holy Spirit, will again blazon the Gospel throughout our land. It may be that this land will see once more the Church of Christ appearing in all her beauty and 'terrible as an army with banners'.[5]

Looking at the situation in the United Kingdom today, after the passage of fifty years, it appears that Mr Murray's predicted alternative of 'strengthening a remnant' is closer to reality. We certainly have not witnessed a general outpouring of the Holy Spirit. Rather, what we are seeing is 'a flood of apostasy, sin and judgement'. Alongside the recovery of the Reformed vision in the 1960s there was a sea change taking place in British society. The decade came to be known as the 'swinging sixties'. Moral restraints were cast off in the interests of creating what was considered to be a 'civilized' society. Secular humanism was on the march. It was no longer possible to speak about absolute truth. Relativism took over. The ideal that was set forth was a pluralist society, where all religions are considered equal. The Christian foundation that made the nation great was undermined and the church was left in the midst of a collapsing culture.

The church had not fully recovered from the liberalism that wasted her for over half a century, before she was invaded by this culture. The evangelicalism that survived gradually under-went a change, as she succumbed to worldliness. David Wells, who so clearly analysed the state of modern evangelicalism in a series of books written in the 1990s, said:

It is because worldliness has the capacity to destroy the very centre of Christian faith — its understanding of the being and character, the acts and truth of God with all the consequences that this has for Christian faithfulness — that we are now seeing such a drastic transformation of evangelical faith.[6]

In the light of what has transpired in recent years it is surely right to ask questions about what good has been achieved by the Reformed recovery and where things might have gone wrong. To seek answers we will attempt to make a tentative assessment as to how much the vision was fulfilled and what factors may have contributed to it being unfulfilled.

A vision fulfilled

1. *We have a record of what God can do through a leader in the most difficult times*

It appeared at the beginning of the century as if liberal theology, with its man-centred outlook, was going to sweep all before it. There were devastating consequences for western Christianity as a result of Higher Criticism, spreading from Germany. As far as the UK was concerned, unlike the two previous centuries, the twentieth century did not witness a major widespread revival. Although opinions differ over the effect of the 1904 Revival in Wales, Dr Lloyd-Jones maintained that it was the people converted at that time who kept the churches in Wales going, even under theologically liberal ministers.[7] This is what he found when he went to Aberavon in 1926. He knew personally many of the leading figures in the 1904 Revival and identified with what was called 'the old Welsh strand' in the revival. Drawing inspiration from the Welsh Calvinistic Methodist fathers and discovering more and more, through literature, a similar heritage elsewhere, he was prepared by God to labour for the dawn of a better day.

Viewing the early ministry of Dr Lloyd-Jones in South Wales, R. B. Jones said, 'He's born out of due time.' During the 1930s and 1940s the Doctor stood almost alone. In the late 1940s and early 1950s he drew some encouragement from the younger men who had begun to discover the Reformed heritage. He saw the recovery of the vision of God in his majesty and glory as the greatest need of the church.

In the words of Iain Murray:

He saw man-centredness — whether in evangelism or in the theological scholarship approved by the secular universities — as the root of modern evangelical weakness, and did not believe churches would see a better day until they learned again to 'cease from man'.[8]

The stature of the man can be gauged from the vacuum that was left in evangelical life in the UK, and especially in England and Wales, by his death in 1981. The church in Britain today is in great need of his kind of leadership.

2. *We have an abiding armoury of Reformed truth*

The Puritan era was undoubtedly the greatest period of reformation and revival ever experienced in England. It produced spiritual giants. There was a peculiar unction on their ministries and this was captured in their writings. In subsequent centuries when God has come to revive his work there has been a 'going back' in mind and heart to the glories of that era.

This was the case with the great evangelist George Whitefield. Some of his writings were published under the title *The Revived Puritan* (1829), of which he said:

The Puritans, though dead, by their writings they yet speak; a peculiar unction attends them to this very hour; and for these thirty years passed I have remarked that the more true and vital religion hath revived either at home or abroad, the more the good old puritanical writings ... have been called for.[9]

We see the same thing occurring again with C. H. Spurgeon. Speaking of the discovery he made in the old manse in Stambourne he said, 'Out of the present contempt into which Puritanism has fallen, many brave hearts and true will fetch it, by the help of God, ere many years have passed.' Towards the end of his life he was regarded as 'the last of the Puritans.' The same thing was repeated in the twentieth century with Dr Lloyd-Jones being described as 'a kind of Puritan.'

If Spurgeon had discovered a 'gold mine' in his day, what riches we possess at the beginning of the twenty-first century![10] Surely there are more than enough substances to ignite sparks of light and life in young men, as it did in Whitefield, Spurgeon and Lloyd-Jones. As a contemporary preacher has put it:

As furnaces burn with ancient coal and not with the leaves that fall from today's trees so my heart is kindled with the fiery substance I find in the old Scripture-steeped sermons of Puritan pastors.[11]

3. *We have witnessed a worldwide spread of Reformed theology*

The full story of how the work inspired by the Doctor's ministry spread to the ends of the earth is beyond the size and scope of this volume. Some of it has already been told; much more has still to be recorded. We have already noted a reference to 'the swelling numbers' in the late 1950s, whose thinking and theology had been changed by the ministry at Westminster Chapel. In paying tribute to the Doctor, James Packer said 'part of his legacy to the world was men — pastors, young and middle-aged, for whom his Puritanism was an inspiration, and he himself, as Americans would say, a role-model'.[12]

It is not surprising that during the 1960s new literature projects came into existence. Outlets for selling Reformed books increased, and ministers began to encourage the setting up of bookstalls in local congregations. Bookselling agents and distributors were established in the United States, South Africa and Australia. Christian Booksellers' Conventions became useful instruments in promoting the new books. Humphrey Mildred of the Banner of Truth Trust began attending the USA Conventions in 1964 and, through the influence of John Reisinger, who has been mentioned already, he was led to the group in Carlisle, Pennsylvania, who had set up Puritan Publications Inc. This resulted in the establishing of a distribution warehouse in Carlisle, to wholesale Banner books in North America. In 1960, through a member of the Banner staff, prompted by reading of Mrs Spurgeon's Book Fund, there was set up the Banner Book Fund which has provided grants to needy pastors and students the world over.

Soon after the first Banner reprints appeared, there was a call for them to be translated into foreign languages. A start was made in Spanish. *The Banner of Truth* magazine in November 1959 carried a news item, 'A New Missionary Enterprise in Spain'. The leaders of the work were two men who had recently graduated from Westminster Theological Seminary, David Estrada and Terry Atkinson. The first volume translated was *Revival Year Sermons* by C. H. Spurgeon, and a magazine, *El Estandarte de la Verdad*, commenced. In July 1960 it was announced that there was an appeal for a Portuguese translation of Alleine's *Alarm to the Unconverted* and so began another sphere that opened fields in South America. From Westminster Chapel, Bill Barkley and Jack Walkey pioneered the gospel and Reformed literature in

Brazil. In France, translation work began under the supervision of the European Missionary Fellowship with the Rev. Bill Clark as the leader.

It was not long before books were reaching into Eastern Europe and Russia, in spite of the 'Iron Curtain'. A pioneer in this field was Colonel Robert Thomson (1886-1967), who had served in the British Foreign Office and knew the languages of Eastern Europe. In 1964 he was accompanied by Julian Sherman-Mouton, a worker at the Banner offices, and they came into contact with a recent convert, Simo Ralevic, to whom they gave *Ecclesiastes* by Charles Bridges. The following year the Colonel, accompanied by Roger Weil, made further contact with Simo, which led to his coming to the Leicester Conference.

In China, another land dominated by Communist ideology, a work had been going on for some years under the auspices of the Reformation Translation Fellowship. As a result of the teaching of Dr J. G. Vos in Manchuria, a native Chinese, Charles Chao, came to an understanding of the Reformed faith and in 1949, in partnership with the Rev. Samuel Boyle, began to translate Reformed titles for the Chinese Church. Translations of works by American and Dutch authors were later supplemented by some of the new Banner titles.

In the early 1970s there came the written ministry of Dr Martyn Lloyd-Jones which has, like Spurgeon's sermons a century earlier, 'encompassed the globe'. Although Dr Lloyd-Jones underwent major surgery in March 1968 he recovered sufficiently to have continued in the pulpit at Westminster Chapel. Instead he retired and gave as an explanation:

What really finally decided me to do this was the feeling that I should bring out in book form some of the material I have gathered over the years and especially what I have tried to do on the Epistle to the Romans.[13]

The first volume of the series on Romans (chapter 3:20 – 4:25 *Atonement and Justification)* appeared in 1970.[14] The fourteenth and final volume was published in 2003. It is some years ago that sales passed the million mark. The Doctor's writings have been translated into many languages. All fourteen volumes of Romans have been translated into Portuguese and Korean.

A vision unfulfilled

If we were asked to focus on a time when that promising 'vision' seemed to falter, we would have to point in the direction of the second half of the 1960s. In retrospect it appears to have been a period of 'partings'. In 1965 the leaders of the Leicester Ministers' Conference parted with their attempts to press on with church reformation. There was a watershed in 1966 when Dr Lloyd-Jones and Dr John Stott were found in open disagreement on the way forward for those who found themselves caught up in doctrinally mixed denominations. In 1968 the Doctor retired from Westminster Chapel. The same year men associated with the Reformed recovery, considering that some of the emphases of the Banner were too Presbyterian-oriented, formed the Carey Conference and associated ministries. Both the Puritan Conference and the Westminster Fellowship had to be reconstituted in 1970, to exclude those remaining in, and sympathetic to, mixed denominations. In the early 1970s some felt a vacuum in the English scene with the removal of Iain Murray and the Banner of Truth Trust to Edinburgh.

Looking back on these developments and seeking to learn some lessons for the future, three things might be considered as vital to the furtherance of the vision.

Leicester Ministers' Conference, 1965

In the centre: Dr D. M. Lloyd-Jones, Iain Murray and John Murray

1. *It is vital to maintain a full-orbed witness to the Reformed faith.*

It is the duty of the church to bear witness to the whole counsel of God. Professor John Murray, in an address on 'The Creedal Basis of Union in the Church' given at the 1965 Leicester Ministers' Conference, asks the question: 'Is it sufficient to have a common denominator confession, general and broad enough, to express the faith of all true evangelicals, but lacking in the specifics on which such evangelicals are divided?' He makes a distinction between voluntary organizations and the church and goes on to say:

> The church is not a voluntary organization; it is a divinely instituted organization of which Christ is the head, the assembly of the covenant people of God, the fellowship of the Spirit, and the body of Christ. The witness given to bear and the confession to be made is the whole counsel of God. There is no restriction that may properly be devised, proposed or imposed. Its faith is the whole revealed counsel of God.[15]

Among the reasons for holding to this view are:

a. To go back on what has been a development of creeds and confessions of faith over the centuries and resort to a more attenuated creedal affirmation is to discard the work of the Holy Spirit in the generations of Christian history. Professor Murray wrote:

> To discard the heritage of the past is the mark of both ignorance and conceit. The way of humility before God and of gratitude to him is to recognize that other men laboured and we have entered into their labours.

b. A full-orbed witness safeguards against the danger of doctrinal indifferentism. Carl Trueman argues that the danger of having minimal statements of faith is that 'important areas of doctrine, such as the sacraments, salvation and the last things are marginalized, relegated to irrelevancies and sometimes all but forgotten'. He asks the pertinent question: 'Once we start ditching our distinctives, where do we stop?' and goes on to claim: 'Indeed the existence of denominations is often a historical witness to the fact that these things are of crucial importance.'[16]

c. The Reformed system of doctrine is, in the words of Professor John Murray, 'to be carefully distinguished from as well as set over against, not only non-Christian systems of thought but also systems of belief that in general terms may be called Christian or even Evangelical.'[17] In speaking about the question of church fellowship in the light of the differences between Reformed theology and Arminianism, Dr J. Gresham Machen said, 'It is difficult to see how anyone who has really studied the question can regard that difference as unimportant. On the contrary, it touches very closely some of the profoundest things of the Christian faith.'[18] 'Arminianism', said C. H. Spurgeon, 'has usually been the route by which Protestants have travelled downward to Socinianism.'

d. Reformed doctrine gives the only ultimate guarantee of success and victory, under the blessing of God. B. B. Warfield's writings are unsurpassed in the contention that Calvinism is the hope of the world. He said: 'Only the Calvinist is the consistent supernaturalist, and only consistent supernaturalism can save supernatural religion for the world.' He saw that the ultimate fight will be between 'a stiff thorough-going orthodoxy and a stiff thorough-going infidelity' (words of H. Boynton Smith). As A. A. Hodge declared: 'The last issue must be between Atheism in its countless forms and Calvinism. The other systems will be crushed as the half-rotten ice between two great bergs.'

2. *It is vital to maintain zeal for church reform*

Dr Packer, speaking of the Puritan dream as it developed under Elizabeth I, James II and Charles I and blossomed in the Interregnum, said: 'Puritanism was essentially a movement for church reform, pastoral renewal and evangelism and spiritual revival; and in addition — indeed as direct expression of its zeal for God's honour — it was a world-view.'[19] The Puritan ideal was to serve God in a Reformed church that would be instrumental in reforming the nation. Protestants who had fled to the Continent under the persecution of Mary's reign saw the Reformed 'ideal' in John Calvin's Geneva — 'the most perfect schole of Christ' on earth. It was concern for the good of the whole church as the body of Christ that lay behind efforts for reform. In the words of the Solemn League and Covenant:

> We shall sincerely, really and constantly, through the grace of God, endeavour in our several places and callings ... the reformation of religion in the kingdoms of England and Ireland, in doctrine, worship, discipline and government, according to the Word of God, and the example of the best Reformed churches.

The human instruments in the change that took place during the course of the twentieth century were individuals such as A. W. Pink and Jay Green; or para-church organizations, like the Christian Unions, the Evangelical Library, the Evangelical Movement of Wales and the Banner of Truth Trust. They all played a vital part in the restoration of Reformed truth but the expectation was that as a result of the new understanding, new church life and order would arise. Church life had sunk to such a low level in some places that, for example, A. W. Pink, who was raised up to exercise a unique ministry for the recovery of the doctrines of free grace, virtually gave up on church association.

But as the long-forgotten scriptural truths were recovered it seemed logical that matters set out in the New Testament pertaining to church unity, order, government and discipline would be implemented.

One place where we might have expected this to take place was at Westminster Chapel. However it is true to say that over the thirty years of the Doctor's ministry, the chapel resembled more a preaching station than a church. The Doctor was the undoubted leader. There was no body of elders and therefore no proper delegation of pastoral responsibilities. The 'church meeting' exercised a decision-making function, despite the fact that in any church meeting numbers present never amounted to as many as half the membership. There was a kind of a 'church within a church'. Iain Murray attributes some of the lack of progress in the chapel to the Doctor's deficiency in organization:

> The problem of turning the Westminster congregation into a true church fellowship concerned him, but its resolution was also hindered, to some degree, by the same lack of organisation. In 1952, for instance, lists were prepared which placed all the members of the church in groups, depending on the location of their homes, in order to introduce 'a suitable system of visitation'. The scheme never came into effective operation. Worse, as Westminster had grown dependent over many years on a strong single leader at the top, it was unprepared for the sudden vacancy in 1968.[20]

What was true of Westminster Chapel was reflected in some ways in the church in England as a whole. There was justifiable concern over the state of the denominations and the need for separation from unbelief. Alongside this was a desire for the expression of evangelical unity over against the ecumenical movement. At the same time there was a measure of disagreement about whether that unity should embrace the Arminian/Calvinist divide. However, in the end the proposed solution did not go beyond a loose kind of association of evangelicals. In an interview with Carl Henry in 1979, the Doctor, in referring to 'mixed denominations', said:

> I believe in *evangelical ecumenism.* I believe Evangelicals should combine forces — not to form a new denomination, but for fellowship and co-operation. Such mutual strengthening is the hopeful way in the future.[21]

Subsequent to the public differences between Stott and Lloyd-Jones at Westminster Central Hall in 1966, the Doctor persuaded the chapel to join the Fellowship of Independent Evangelical Churches (FIEC) and by so doing became a member of the British Evangelical Council (BEC), which came to great prominence in the 1970s.

It is clear that the way of trying to unite evangelicals by common adherence to a minimum of essential scriptural truths has not been a success. The only way that this can be done is through the restoration of a fuller, stronger testimony to the Word of God and to the New Testament concept of the church. She has been formed as a visible, corporate entity under the Headship of Christ and in submission to his Word as her only rule. She has no authority to limit her corporate testimony to the truths essential to be believed in order to be saved. Are the doctrines of Calvinism integral to New Testament Christianity? Is the teaching on government, worship and ministry vital to the well-being of the church? If we are convinced they are, we will hold to them and seek that the church be restored as near as possible to the pattern set out in Scripture. It is in those ages when the churches have sought most thoroughly to adhere to the whole testimony of Scripture that we have seen the clearest examples of unity, notably the Reformation and Puritan eras. We find practical wisdom in words written by the eminent theologian, R. L. Dabney:

> The only practicable scheme of church association is that which unites in one denomination those who are honestly agreed, while it leaves all others who differ from them the same liberty of association and testimony. Does a certain part of the visible catholic church result? I answer it is the least of the possible evils.

3. *It is vital to recover the creation and covenant view of the family.*

Perhaps another explanation why the vision did not make further progress is that it did not reach down to the level of the family in the way that it did in the Puritan era. The Puritans (in England, Scotland, Holland and New England) crusaded for a high view of the family, proclaiming it both as the basic unit of society and a little church in itself, with the head of the house as its minister and his wife as his assistant. One of the early Puritans, Richard Greenham, declared: 'If ever we would have the Church of God to continue among us we must bring it into our households and nourish it in our families.' Richard Baxter, whose methods of instruction in families transformed the spiritual condition of Kidderminster, said, 'Holy families must be the chief preservers of religion in the world.' The Puritans sought to reform family life according to biblical principles. According to Dr Packer, 'They were the creators of the English Christian marriage, the English Christian family and the English Christian home.'

In the booklet referred to above, Carl Trueman says:

> Not only must we make sure that the focal point of our church is the doctrinal preaching of the gospel in all

its fulness, we must also make sure that this doctrine penetrates to the pew. The history of the church is peppered with examples of churches which enjoyed powerful, faithful preaching for many years and yet which all but collapsed into doctrinal apathy and even heresy on the retirement or death of their minister. While a number of reasons could be given for this, one underlying factor has to be the failure of the message to pass effectively from the pulpit to the pew.[22]

As believers in the doctrine of creation and in covenant theology, Reformed Christians, whatever our view on baptism, must place greater emphasis on the solidarity of the family. The family is a God-given pattern and forms an essential feature of God's created order. The created order of the family is not ignored but taken up in God's redemptive provision. How good it would be to see that vision restored to church life today!

Our hope

The Reformed faith has had a wonderful history. We have seen a recovery of it in the last fifty years. It is destined to have a glorious future. If our longed-for desires for the restoration of the church in Britain to her former glories have not been fulfilled we must not faint in the present day of adversity. 'For the vision is yet for an appointed time; but at the end it will speak, and it will not lie. Though it tarries, wait for it; because it will surely come, it will not tarry' (Habakkuk 2:3).

It is appropriate that the closing word should be from the writings of my namesake to whom, under God, I owe so much.

Faith imbued with zeal for the honour of Christ and the glory of God will have no sympathy with the defeatism which is, after all, but disguised fatalism. He who is head over all things is head over all things to his body the church. He has all authority in heaven and in earth. And he is the Lord of the Spirit. Implicit in the prayer he taught his disciples to pray, 'thy will be done as in heaven so in earth', is the prayer that the whole earth should be filled with his praise. Nothing less is the measure of the believer's desire. 'And blessed be his glorious name for ever; and let the whole earth be filled with his glory.'[23]

Chronology of
the Reformed recovery

1899   D. M. Lloyd-Jones born
1903   Geoffrey Williams converted
1914   Lloyd-Jones given a copy of *Life of Howell Harris*
1918   Pink's *Sovereignty of God* published
1919   First University Christian Union conference in London
1925   Geoffrey Williams begins to collect books for a library
1925   Lloyd-Jones begins reading the Puritans
1927   D. M. Lloyd-Jones and goes to South Wales
1928   The founding of Inter-Varsity Fellowship
1929   The founding of Westminster Theological Seminary
1929   *The Evangelical Quarterly* launched
1931   Iain Murray born
1933   Establishment of Beddington Free Grace Library
1938   Lloyd-Jones comes to Westminster Chapel
1941   Beginnings of Westminster Fellowship
1943   Lloyd-Jones becomes sole pastor at Westminster
        Chapel
1944   James Packer converted
1945   John Stott becomes curate at All Souls
1945   Evangelical Library established in London
1945   Tyndale Hall, Cambridge, opened

1948 *Y Cyclhgrawn Efengylaidd* issued
1949 Calvin's *Institutes* reprinted
1950 19-20 December — the first Puritan Conference
1951 Third IVF Conference in Wales
1952 Publication of *The Way, the Truth and the Life* in the USA
1953 John Murray gives Evangelical Library Lecture in London
1953 *The New Bible Commentary* published
1954 Iain Murray prepares for the ministry
1954 Jay Green begins Sovereign Grace Book Club
1955 *The Evangelical Magazine of Wales* issued in March
1955 *The Banner of Truth* magazine issued in September
1955 D. J. W. Cullum converted
1956 Iain Murray becomes assistant to Dr Lloyd-Jones
1957 The Banner of Truth Trust established
1957 First two Banner reprints appear
1958 Banner moves to 78b Chiltern Street
1959 *Evangelical Magazine* launched
1961 Iain Murray inducted to Grove Chapel
1962 First Leicester Ministers' Conference
1966 The Lloyd-Jones/Stott confrontation at Westminster Central Hall
1967 Evangelical Press begun by Robin Bird
1967 First issue of *Evangelical Times*
1968 Close of Dr Lloyd-Jones' ministry at Westminster Chapel
1970 The end of the Puritan Conference
1971 Start of the Westminster Conference
1972 The Banner moves headquarters to Edinburgh
1972 Iain Murray accepted into Free Church ministry
1975 The death of John Murray
1978 First Banner of Truth Ministers' Conference in the USA
1981 The death of Dr Lloyd-Jones

Chronology of
John Murray 1898-1975

1898   Born in Badbea
1909   Begins secondary education at Dornoch Academy
1917   Called up and joins the Black Watch
1918   Wounded in action; loses right eye
1923   Graduated from Glasgow University
1923   Began theological studies with FP Church — Rev.
         Donald Beaton
1924   Goes to Princeton Seminary to study
1927   Graduates Bachelor and Master of Theology
1928   Studies at New College, Edinburgh University
1929   Assistant to C. W. Hodge in Princeton Seminary
1930   Accepts Instructor in Theology at Westminster
         Seminary
1935   Visit to Scotland
1936   Formation of Orthodox Presbyterian Church, USA
1936   Chairman for the Propagation of the Reformed Faith in
         New England
1937   Ordained to the ministry in the OPC
1937   Accepts Professorship of Systematic Theology at
         Westminster
1939   Visit to Scotland

1942   Death of his father
1945   Visit to Scotland
1948   At funeral of Principal John MacLeod
1953   Evangelical Library Lecture on 'Reformation Principles'
1953   TSF Cambridge 'The Covenant of Grace'.
1953   Summer School, Cambridge: 'Limited atonement'
1953   Reformed Ecumenical Synod in Edinburgh
1953   Preached in Carnegie Hall, Dornoch
1955   November 'Sabbatical' — 'my 22nd crossing'
1956   22 Jan Preaches in Free St Columba's, Edinburgh
1956   April Preaches in Dornoch Free Church
1958   Speaking in London to EPF on Presbyterian
        Government
1958   Campbell Morgan Bible Lecture 'The Heavenly Priestly
        Activity of Christ'
1960   *Commentary on Romans,* vol. 1 published
1962   2-5 July, First Ministers' Conference at Leicester
1964   Home for three months
1964   13-17 July Second Leicester Conference
1965   7 months leave
1965   5-8 April Third Leicester Conference
1965   27 April RTF meeting in Edinburgh
1965   *Commentary on Romans,* Vol. 2 published
1966   Retires from Westminster Seminary
1967   Marries Valerie Knowlton
1968   Logan born
1969   Last visit to USA
1971   Anne-Margaret born
1971   Attends his last Leicester Conference
1972   Supply preacher at Ardgay Free Church
1975   Illness and death

Notes

Chapter 1

1. C. H. Spurgeon, *An All-round Ministry* (1900, reprint, Edinburgh, Banner of Truth Trust, 1960), p.360.
2. *Later Letters of Marcus Dods* (London, Hodder and Stoughton, 1911), p.67.
3. B. B. Warfield, *Calvin as a Theologian and Calvinism Today* (Edinburgh, Hope Trust, 1909), pp.14-15.
4. Douglas Johnson, *Contending for the Faith* (Leicester, IVP, 1979), p.61.
5. 'Testimony for the Truth in the British Universities' in *The Evangelical Quarterly*, Oct. 1933, pp.338-41.
6. A. Rendle Short, *Modern Discovery and the Bible* (London, IVF, 1952), p.230.
7. E. J. Poole-Connor, *Evangelicalism in England* (London, FIEC, 1951), p.251.
8. S. M. Houghton, *My Life & Books* (Edinburgh, Banner, 1988), p.6.
9. *C. H. Spurgeon: the Early Years* (London, Banner, 1962), pp.10-11.
10. *Evangelical Quarterly*, Vol. 1, No. 1, January 1929 (London, James Clarke, 1929), p.3.

Chapter 2

1. Geraint Fielder, *Lord of the Years* (Leicester, IVP, 1988), p.245.
2. Johnson, *Contending for the Faith*, p.13.

3. In later years the title was shortened to 'Inter-Varsity Fellowship of Evangelical Unions' with a general use of the initials 'IVF'. In the 1970s it was accepted that the contraction 'inter-varsity' had gone out of fashion, so in 1975 the overall name was changed to 'Universities and Colleges Christian Fellowship' with the initials 'UCCF' becoming the accepted designation.

4. David G. Fountain, *Contending for the Faith: E. J. Poole-Connor* (London, Wakeman Trust, 2005), p.48.

5. Iain H. Murray, *D. M. Lloyd-Jones: the Fight of Faith* (Edinburgh, Banner, 1990), p.306.

6. Fountain, *Contending for the Faith*, p.153.

7. I. H. Murray, *The Life of Arthur W Pink* (Edinburgh, Banner, 2004), p.47.

8. Arthur W. Pink, *Letters from Spartanburg 1917-1920* (Columbia, Richbarry Press, 1993), p.102.

9. Jay Green web site.

10. *The Banner of Truth*, No. 3, October 1956, p.19. Mr Watson became assistant to David Fountain at Spring Road Evangelical Church in Southampton and carried on the agency for SGBC from what became a familiar address to those beginning to appreciate the doctrines of grace: '1 Cliff House, Weston Lane, Southampton'. The demand for the books often exceeded the supply. Mr Watson also held stocks of the books and booklets of A. W. Pink. This was the means of introducing Pink to a new readership and increased the desire for similar teaching.

11. There is a reference to the SGU in a letter of Dr Lloyd-Jones written in 1953: 'I am denounced as a dangerous Arminian by a Society of Hyper-Calvinists here in London because in my pamphlet on the *Presentation of the Gospel* I teach that a free offer of salvation should be made to all in preaching'. *D Martyn Lloyd-Jones Letters 1919-1981* (Edinburgh, Banner, 1994), p.189.

12. Walter Chantry, 'Building a New Work', *The Banner of Truth*, No. 469, p.7.

13. For more on this see Geoffrey Thomas, *Ernest C. Reisinger: a Biography* (Edinburgh, Banner, 2002).

14. Iain Murray, 'Greatly Loved Christian Leader Goes Home', *The Banner of Truth*, No. 241.

15. *Record of the Trial of the Rev. Prof. J. E. Davey* (published by authority of the General Assembly, Belfast, 1927).

16. John Grier in a letter to the author.

17. Mr Doggett records an early connection with Iain Murray: 'In the summer of that year (1955) the writer was preaching at Oxford. In his congregation was a young graduate, Iain Murray. A few weeks later he received through the post No. 1 of *The Banner of Truth*' (*Grace*, May 2002, p.9).

Chapter 3

1. *Evangelical Quarterly*, Vol. 1, No. 1, January 1929 (London, James Clarke, 1929), p.3.
2. Addresses at the Annual Meeting of the Evangelical Library, 1955, p.14.
3. Addresses etc, 1956, p.13.
4. Iain H. Murray, *D M Lloyd-Jones: the First Forty Years 1899-1939* (Edinburgh, Banner, 1982), p.27.
5. D. M. Lloyd-Jones, *Preaching and Preachers* (London, Hodder, 1971), p.146.
6. Murray, *D M Lloyd-Jones: the First Forty Years*, p.64.
7. D. M. Lloyd-Jones, *The Puritans: Their Origins and Successors* (Edinburgh, Banner, 1987), p.237.
8. Related by J. Elwyn Davies, 'God's Gift to a Nation' in *Martyn Lloyd-Jones: Chosen by God*, edited by Christopher Catherwood (Highland Books, 1986), p.179.
9. An interview by Carl Henry in *Martyn Lloyd-Jones: Chosen by God*, p.97.
10. Related by J. Elwyn Davies, 'God's Gift to a Nation' in *Martyn Lloyd-Jones: Chosen by God*, p.180.
11. Murray, *D M Lloyd-Jones: the First Forty Years*, pp.253-4.
12. As above, p.287.
13. Included in *Evangelistic Sermons at Aberavon* (Edinburgh, Banner, 1983), p.259.
14. J. Elwyn Davies, 'God's Gift to a Nation' in *Martyn Lloyd-Jones: Chosen by God*, p.183.
15. Murray, *D. M. Lloyd-Jones: the Fight of Faith*, pp.208-9.

Chapter 4

1. Carl Henry in *Martyn Lloyd-Jones: Chosen by God*, p.98.
2. *D. Martyn Lloyd-Jones Letters 1919-1981* (Edinburgh, Banner, 1994), p.70.

3. Gaius Davies in *Martyn Lloyd-Jones: Chosen by God,* p.65.
4. Geraint Fielder, *Lord of the Years* (Leicester, IVP, 1988), pp.60-61.
5. Murray, *D M Lloyd-Jones: the Fight of Faith*, p.183.
6. As above, p.154.
7. Geraint D. Fielder, *Excuse me, Mr Davies — Hallelujah!* (Bryntirion, E P of Wales, 1983), p.31.
8. As above, p.108.
9. As above, p.132.
10. Noel Gibbard, *The First Fifty Years* (Bryntirion, E P of Wales, 2002), p.21.
11. As above, p.27.
12. As above, pp.28-30. A magazine in English, *The Evangelical Magazine of Wales,* was produced in 1955.
13. Fielder, *Excuse me, Mr Davies — Hallelujah!* p.157.
14. As above, p.157.
15. As above, p.158.
16. *D. Martyn Lloyd-Jones Letters 1919-1981*, p.62.
17. *Martyn Lloyd-Jones: Chosen by God,* p.226.
18. Murray, *D. M. Lloyd-Jones: the Fight of Faith 1939-1981*, p.774.

Chapter 5

1. *Eternal Truth,* vol. 3, no.2, April/June 1961, p.14.
2. Geoffrey Williams, *Addresses at Evangelical Library,* 1956, p.1.
3. Report at Annual Meeting, 1961, p.14.
4. See S. M. Houghton, *My Life & Books* (Edinburgh, Banner, 1988), p.143, and *The Banner of Truth,* No. 137, February 1957, pp.28-29. Mr Houghton was reporting on the Annual Meeting of the Evangelical Library on 10 December 1974, at which there was a Farewell to Mr Williams. He records: 'The present writer, who attended the valedictory meeting, had the secret pleasure of supposing he was the only person present at the meeting who had attended week-evening meetings at the Brandries in the far-off days [1924] when the book collection was in its infancy'. Mr Houghton informs us that Mr Williams was 'by earthly calling a member of the banking fraternity'.
5. Quoted in Iain Murray, *Not a Museum, But a living Force* (Evangelical Library, 1995), p.2.

6. This testimony is given by Mr Williams when he is recording the passing of Mr Bliss in the *Evangelical Library Bulletin,* Spring 1971, p.22.
7. Murray, *D M Lloyd-Jones: The Fight of Faith,* p.82.
8. *D. Martyn Lloyd-Jones Letters 1919-1981,* pp.53-54.
9. Murray, *D M Lloyd-Jones: The Fight of Faith,* p.84.
10. Ernest Kevan, *Evangelical Quarterly,* July 1945.
11. Murray, *D M Lloyd-Jones: The Fight of Faith,* p.199 and p.759 fn.
12. *Evangelical Library Bulletin,* Autumn 1959.

Chapter 6

1. Alister McGrath, *To Know and Serve God: Life of James Packer* (London, Hodder, 1997), p.6.
2. Christopher Catherwood, *Five Evangelical Leaders* (London, Hodder, 1984), p.170.
3. 'The Spirit with the Word: the Reformation Revivalism of George Whitefield' in J. I. Packer, *Selected Shorter Writings,* vol. 4, p.42.
4. Packer's growing appreciation of the Puritans and those who had been influenced by them, such as J. C. Ryle, led him to voice his criticism of the Keswick movement's teaching. He believed that a book published in 1952, *So Great Salvation* by Steven Barabbas, gave a new lease of life to the old Keswick errors. He countered this book with an extended critical review of it in *The Evangelical Quarterly,* July 1955. He argued that the Keswick teaching was Pelagian, in that it diminished the role of God and falsely elevated the role of human will and freedom. The review evoked strong reaction and there was a threat even to Packer's position as lecturer at Tyndale Hall, Bristol. Alister McGrath comments: 'It is widely agreed that Packer's review marked the end of the dominance of the Keswick approach among younger evangelicals. Looking back it can be argued that this review simultaneously established Packer as something of a hero with an emerging younger generation of evangelicals who were dissatisfied with the uncritical Pietism of British evangelicalism at this period, and alienated an older generation within the evangelical establishment of the day', *To Know and Serve God: Life of James Packer,* p.79.
5. Murray, *D M Lloyd-Jones: The Fight of Faith,* p.188. British restaurants were institutions introduced during the Second World War to supply plain food.

6. Packer, quoted in Murray, *The Fight of Faith*, p.187.
7. Packer, quoted in Murray, *The Fight of Faith*, p.188.
8. Christopher Catherwood, *Martyn Lloyd-Jones: Chosen by God*, pp.36-37.
9. *The Christian Graduate*, June and September 1950.
10. Packer quoted in Murray, *The Fight of Faith*, p.227.
11. See Alister McGrath, *To Know and Serve God: Life of James Packer*, p.52; and David Fountain in *Puritan Principles: Puritan Papers 1951-54* (Tentmaker Publications), pp.5-6.
12. *Puritan Principles: Puritan Papers 1951-54*, p.5.
13. *A Goodly Heritage* (London, Banner, 1959), p.2.
14. David Fountain in *Puritan Principles*, p.8.
15. Murray, *The Fight of Faith*, p.231.
16. McGrath, *To Know and Serve God: Life of James Packer*, p.53.

Chapter 7

1. Tom Rees died in 1970 at the early age of fifty-eight. Iain Murray paid tribute to him in *The Banner of Truth* magazine, May 1970. He sought to assess the changes that had taken place in his lifetime and concluded: 'In future years, when the old theology will have come again into its own, we trust that it will not be forgotten that God used Tom Rees to lay hold of men who were to take part in this change of direction in the mid-twentieth century. For the present writer, and his wife, the year of meeting Mr Rees was the year of salvation and we will not cease to be thankful for the privilege of having known him.'
2. Murray, *D M Lloyd-Jones: The Fight of Faith*, p.193.
3. Murray, *The Banner of Truth*, No. 200, May 1980, p.4.
4. Murray, *The Banner of Truth*, No. 362.
5. 'The Rev. James Shiphardson was a Methodist minister in Durham City, England, whom I never knew personally, but whose copy of the two-volume British edition of Edwards (then a rarity in the second-hand market) I received from his daughter on May 21, 1952.' From the preface to *Jonathan Edwards: A New Biography* by Iain Murray (Edinburgh, Banner, 1987), p.xii.
6. Murray, *The Banner of Truth*, No. 510, March 2006, p.13.
7. Murray, *The Banner of Truth*, No. 200, May 1980, p.6.
8. Murray, *The Fight of Faith*, p.355.
9. *The Banner of Truth*, September 1955, p.20.

10. Murray, *The Fight of Faith*, p.355.
11. *D Martyn Lloyd-Jones Letters 1919-1981* (Edinburgh, Banner, 1994).
12. *My Life and Books: Reminiscences of S M Houghton* (Edinburgh, Banner, 1988), p.141.
13. As above, p.143.
14. Murray, *The Fight of Faith*, p.356.
15. Erroll Hulse, in an e-mail to the author.
16. Erroll Hulse, *Reformation Today*, No. 216, p.30.
17. Letter from Peter Golding.

Chapter 8

1. One of the ministers who came to discover the deficiencies of the type of crusade evangelism was the Rev. William Still. He was inducted to a congregation of the Church of Scotland which was threatened with closure — Gilcomston South in Aberdeen. Having experimented with evangelistic and youth rallies on Saturday evenings he took the decision to replace them with a prayer meeting. This was the beginning of a turnaround in the life of the church. He began systematic expository preaching and exercised a fruitful ministry for thirty-eight years in Gilcomston. Students were converted and many of his young men, among the first, the brothers James and George Philip and later Sinclair Ferguson, went into the ministry. He became a father figure and leader of the 'Crieff Fellowship' of ministers. His influence did much to stem the tide of liberalism within the Church of Scotland. This movement, which in some ways paralleled what was going on in England, was of a somewhat different character and an assessment of the success and failure of it would require a study on its own.
2. Mr MacRae had been a minister of the Free Church of Scotland since 1915 and was then pastor of the largest Presbyterian congregation in the United Kingdom. For more on this, see *Diary of Kenneth MacRae*, edited by Iain H. Murray (Edinburgh, Banner, 1980). This was one of the books appreciated by the Doctor in the final year of his life — 'I am enjoying it tremendously' (*The Fight of Faith*, p.741).
3. Iain H. Murray, *Life of John Murray* in *Collected Writings of John Murray*, vol. 3 (Edinburgh, Banner, 1982), p.5.

4. Murray, *Life of John Murray* in *Collected Writings*, p.11.
5. Ned B. Stonehouse, *J Gresham Machen: a Biographical Memoir* (1955), p.310.
6. Printed by the Northern Counties Newspaper and Printing and Publishing Co. 1936.
7. Edwin King recalls how he and others 'found the lecture on "the Covenant" heavy going' (*Life*, pp.128-9). Covenant theology was virtually unknown in England at this date. In fact Murray's booklet can be regarded as the beginning of an interest which has grown steadily over fifty years.
8. Murray, *Life of John Murray* in *Collected Writings*, p.129.
9. *Collected Writings of John Murray*, vol. 1 (Edinburgh, Banner, 1982), p.143. It is interesting to note that Murray was not alone in his assessment. Dr Philip E. Hughes, writing in *Christianity Today* in 1959, while welcoming the changes in the theological climate due to the printed page, went on to say: 'Evangelical preaching, however, still leaves much to be desired, especially as there is a deficiency of emphasis on the absolute sovereignty of Almighty God, as Creator, Redeemer and Judge over all the affairs of the world. This means a concomitant deficiency in the view of man and his ability' (reprinted in *International Reformed Bulletin*, April 1959).
10. *Diary of Kenneth MacRae* (Edinburgh, Banner, 1980), p.477.
11. Murray, *Life of John Murray* in *Collected Writings*, p.133.
12. It is worth recording the verdict of Dr J. I. Packer on him: 'Had John Murray been blessed with the luminous literary grace of a C. S. Lewis, or the punchy rhetoric of a Charles Hodge, his name would have been up in lights for the past half-century as the finest Reformed theologian of our time. Unfortunately his genius was not in his prose style; his readers have always found him tough sledding. Also he interacted mainly with older literature, so that those for whom history was bunk and who wanted only snappy comments on the latest theological fads and fancies had to go elsewhere. Few have yet appreciated him at his true worth.'

Chapter 9

1. Iain Murray, 'In the Twentieth Year', *The Banner of Truth*, No. 159, December 1975.
2. Murray, *D Martyn Lloyd-Jones: The Fight of Faith*, p.360.

3. *The Banner of Truth*, No. 399, December 1996, pp.1-4.
4. Erroll Hulse in an e-mail to the author.
5. *The Banner of Truth*, bound, Vol. 1 (Edinburgh, Banner, 1960).
6. David Wells, *No Place for Truth* (Leicester, IVP, 1993) and *God in the Wasteland* (Leicester, IVP, 1994).
7. From notes of an address given by Dr Lloyd-Jones on 'Religious Life in Wales at the turn of this century'.
8. Murray, *The Banner of Truth*, No. 510, March 2006, p.13.
9. Recommendatory preface to *The Works of John Bunyan*, 1767.
10. A recent major work entitled *Meet the Puritans* by Joel Beeke and Randall J. Pederson (Reformation Heritage Books, Grand Rapids, 2006) contains not only the lives of all the leading Puritans but also the details of the writings of these men which have been reprinted since 1950. So many of these works are also available on CD or on the Internet.
11. Dr John Piper in commendation of *Meet the Puritans* (Reformation Heritage Books, 2006).
12. 'A Kind of Puritan' in *Martyn Lloyd-Jones: Chosen by God* (Highland Books, 1986), p.56.
13. *The Banner of Truth*, No. 510, March 2006, p.28.
14. I have a diary entry for 24 July 1970 which reads 'Had one of the most encouraging days in the history of the Trust. Dr Lloyd-Jones came in about 11.30 am and spent the rest of the day at the office. IHM and JJM working with him on the first volume of his series on Romans. Discussed the size of each volume and agreed to the Doctor's proposal that we do chapters 3.20 to 8.4 in 4 vols instead of 3...'
15. John Murray, *Collected Writings*, vol. 1, pp.280-7.
16. Carl Trueman, *Christianity, Liberalism and the New Evangelicalism* (Bristol, Onesimus Books, 2002), p.10.
17. David Van Drunen, *The Pattern of Sound Doctrine* (Phillipsburgh, P & R, 2004), p.231.
18. J. Gresham Machen, *Christianity and Liberalism* (Grand Rapids, Eerdmans, reprint 1981), p.51.
19. Packer, *Among God's Giants* (Kingsway 1991), p.32.
20. Murray, *The Fight of Faith*, p.757. Iain Murray, in speaking about the complexity of the Doctor's make-up, refers to what he implied about himself: 'The South Walian's laziness, plus his genius, makes him despise committees. He is not concerned with carrying things out.'

21. Interview with Carl Henry in *Martyn Lloyd-Jones: Chosen by God*, pp.103-104.
22. Carl Trueman, *Christianity, Liberalism and the New Evangelicalism* (Bristol, Onesimus Books, 2002), p.11.
23. *Collected Writings of John Murray*, vol. 2, p.350.

Select bibliography

Barclay, Oliver. *Evangelicalism in Britain 1935-1995* (Leicester, IVP, 1997).

Beeke, Joel, and Pederson, Randall, *Meet the Puritans* (Grand Rapids, Reformation Heritage Books, 2006).

Fielder, Geraint D. *Excuse me, Mr Davies — Hallelujah!* (Bryntirion, Evangelical Press of Wales, 1983).

Fielder, Geraint. *Lord of the Years* (Leicester, Inter-varsity Press, 1988).

Fountain, David G. *Contending for the Faith: E J Poole-Connor* (London, Wakeman Trust, 2005).

Fountain, David G. *Puritan Principles*: *Puritan Papers 1951-54* (Tentmaker Publications).

Gibbard, Noel. *The First Fifty Years: the History of the Evangelical Movement of Wales* (Bryntirion, Evangelical Press of Wales, 2002).

Houghton, S. M. *My Life & Books* (Edinburgh, Banner of Truth Trust, 1988).

Johnson, Douglas. *Contending for the Faith* (Leicester, IVP, 1979).

McGrath, Alister. *To Know and Serve God: The Life of James I. Packer* (London, Hodder & Stoughton, 1997).

Murray, Iain H. *Life of John Murray* (Edinburgh, Banner of Truth Trust, reprint 2007).

Murray, Iain H. *The Life of Arthur W Pink* (Edinburgh, Banner of Truth Trust, reprint 2004).

Murray, Iain H. *D M Lloyd-Jones: The Fight of Faith* (Edinburgh, Banner of Truth Trust, 1990).

Murray, Iain H. *D M Lloyd-Jones: the First Forty Years 1899-1939* (Edinburgh, Banner of Truth Trust, 1982).

Murray, Iain H. *Not a Museum But a living Force* (Evangelical Library, 1995).

Murray, John. *Collected Writings of John Murray,* 4 volumes (Edinburgh, Banner of Truth Trust, 1976-1982).

Packer, J. I. *Among God's Giants: Aspects of Puritan Christianity* (Eastbourne, Kingsway, 1991).

Poole-Connor, E. J. *Evangelicalism in England* (London, FIEC, 1951).

Diary of Kenneth A MacRae (Edinburgh, Banner of Truth Trust, 1980).

The Banner of Truth magazine

Westminster/Puritan Conference Papers

Index

Index

Index

Index

A wide range of Christian books is available from Evangelical Press. If you would like a free catalogue please write to us or contact us by e-mail. Alternatively, you can view the whole catalogue online at our website:

www.evangelicalpress.org.

Evangelical Press
Faverdale North, Darlington, Co. Durham, DL3 0PH, England

e-mail: sales@evangelicalpress.org

Evangelical Press USA
P. O. Box 825, Webster, New York 14580, USA

e-mail: usa.sales@evangelicalpress.org